THIS NOBLE EDIFICE

A History of Religious & Spiritual Life
at Carleton College
1866–2016

"...it is good that the new era should be marked by the erection of this noble edifice whose splendid tower commands the campus and, indeed, the whole region around; a building designed to express and develop the spirit of Carleton..."

The Rev. John Gardner at the dedication of
Skinner Memorial Chapel, October 8, 1916

THIS NOBLE EDIFICE

A History of Religious & Spiritual Life
at Carleton College
1866–2016

Bruce William Colwell

CARLETON COLLEGE
NORTHFIELD, MINNESOTA

ISBN 978-0-9613911-3-3

Book Design by Mark F. Heiman

This manuscript was made possible in part by the people of Minnesota through a grant funded by an appropriation to the Minnesota Historical Society from the Minnesota Historical & Cultural Heritage Fund. Any views, findings, opinions, conclusions or recommendations expressed in this manuscript are those of the authors and do not necessarily represent those of the State of Minnesota, the Minnesota Historical Society, or the Minnesota Historic Resources Advisory Committee.

Publisher's Cataloging-In-Publication Data:

Names: Colwell, Bruce William, 1950-
Title: This Noble Edifice: A History of Religious and Spiritual Life at Carleton, 1866–2016 / Bruce William Colwell.
Description: Northfield, Minnesota : Carleton College, 2016.
Summary: This history of the Carleton Skinner Chapel and the college chaplaincy chronicles the story of an iconic campus building and the evolution of the place of religion and student spiritual life at Carleton College, a national residential liberal arts college in Northfield, Minnesota.
Identifiers: ISBN 9780961391133
Subjects: Carleton College (Northfield, Minn.) — Religion — History. | College students — Religious life — Minnesota — Northfield — 19th century. | College students — Religious life — Minnesota — Northfield — 20th century. | College students — Religious life — Minnesota — Northfield — 21st century. | College chaplains — Minnesota — Northfield. | Chapels — Minnesota — Northfield. | Universities and colleges — Religion — United States.
Classification: LCC BR561.C847 C65 2016

Contents

Acknowledgments

Although the October 2016 celebration of Carleton College's Skinner Memorial Chapel's centennial anniversary provided the impetus for writing this history of religion at Carleton, it was immediately evident that the history of the historic, iconic Skinner Chapel, while significant, was only a chapter in a larger more important story: the evolving place of religion and the chaplaincy at one of America's premier liberal arts colleges. Thus this history recognizes three interrelated Carleton anniversaries — the institution's 150th, the Skinner Chapel's 100th, and the college chaplaincy's 70th.

For assistance and support with the creation of this book I am grateful and indebted to:

   Tom Lamb, Eric Hillemann, and Nat Wilson in the Carleton College Archives

   David Grabitske and Melinda Hutchinson at the Minnesota Historical Society

   Bardwell Smith, Professor of Religion and Asian Studies, Emeritus, Carleton College

   Louis Newman, Professor of Religion, Carleton College

   Jeanne Halgren Kilde, Director, Religious Studies Program, University of Minnesota, and Jeff Sauve, Associate Archivist, St. Olaf College for helpful and insightful critical reviews of the manuscript

   Nancy Ashmore, editor

A special thanks to:

   Carleton Chaplain Carolyn Fure-Slocum, for encouragement and inspiration, and patience describing the complexity and challenges of the 21st century liberal arts college chaplaincy.

   Mark Heiman for expert editing, image selection, and design that enlivened the text and enhanced its readability; to the extent that this publication reads well and looks good, Mark deserves the credit.

   The Carleton College Sesquicentennial Planning Committee

   The Minnesota Clean Water Land and Legacy Amendment's Arts and Cultural Heritage Fund

Preface

IN THE FEBRUARY 1916 *Alumni Magazine* Carleton Professor of Mental and Moral Philosophy John E. Boodin wrote with eager anticipation of the completion of the construction of the Skinner Memorial Chapel. The new $100,000 English Gothic-style Bedford stone building, he predicted, would stand out as one of the "finest of its kind" among American colleges and with its architecture and location would visually "dominate" the campus and, most significantly, form a "fitting symbol" for the unity of student and campus intellectual, spiritual, and physical life as well as "form a suitable home for Carleton's rich collective life."[1] Student life at Carleton and the early twentieth-century American liberal arts college was, Boodin asserted, a community experience, a common life, in which a proper moral and religious atmosphere was combined with intellectual preparation and physical development. Religion was central and essential to a Carleton education, he continued, and Carleton had "always stood out by virtue of the soundness of its inner life." The spiritual bond which permeated community life was not an "affected piety put on for Sunday wear," but rather a "rugged and wholesome religion." Boodin also commended Carleton's President Donald Cowling, who held a PhD and a divinity degree from Yale, for understanding the fundamental importance of religion and of the new chapel for his small residential liberal arts college.

Carleton's Skinner Memorial Chapel celebrates its centennial anniversary in October 2016. This history of the Carleton chapel and chaplaincy chronicles the story of a building and the evolution of the place of religion and student spiritual life at Carleton College, a national selective residential liberal arts college in Northfield, Minnesota. The central place of religion at Carleton College was implicit in the details of its founding and explicit in the pages of early college catalogs which declared that the school, while unsectarian in its aim, was "intended to be emphatically a Christian College."[2] Carleton, though under no ecclesiastical control, took as its purpose "to provide an education liberal and thorough, embracing moral culture as well as mental discipline; and securing a symmetrical Christian character." The college's 1875 catalog proclaimed the school's intent to be "a true Christian College — not denominational, but distinctly and earnestly evangelical." Consequently, when Carleton's third president, Donald J. Cowling, launched a campaign to enlarge the college's facilities, a beautiful chapel large enough to hold the entire academic community was on the top of the list.

The centrality of religion and the college chapel was characteristic of the late nineteenth- and early twentieth-century American liberal arts college. Historian George P. Schmidt declared that education in colonial America was "the child of religion."[3] Harvard Chaplain Peter J. Gomes noted that the most prominent architectural feature of religiously affiliated liberal arts colleges was the college chapel, "declaiming in wood or stone the central place accorded the public expression of religion in the life of the school" and that the campus design "reflected complementary sitings of the chapel and the library, temples to the twin values of faith and reason by which Christian education in the West has for so long been guided."[4]

This history of Carleton's chapel and chaplaincy is set in this context — a college, founded by the Congregational Conference of Minnesota, that described itself as a Christian college from its 1866 founding through the 1950s. But Carleton was founded as an independent, though church-affiliated, college, where the classical liberal arts curriculum was clearly dominant, a benefactor of the 1828 Yale Report's powerful argument for humanism, the liberal arts, and mental discipline to define the American liberal arts college.[5] The place of religion at Carleton will also be examined in the context of the residential liberal arts college. As the college was also the students' home and the faculty acted *in loco parentis*, the chapel was the student's home church and the chaplain served as the college student's minister.

Alaska Pacific University President F. Thomas Trotter has noted the "profoundly religious origins of schools of learning. The fact is that learning and its institutions are inventions of the religious spirit… Christian thought may be understood as the history of reflection on the nature and uses of knowledge."[6] The nineteenth-century understanding of the liberal arts college was built on this unity of faith and learning. Carleton's first three presidents, James Strong (1870–1903), William Sallmon (1903–1908), and Donald Cowling (1909–1945) each were ordained Protestant ministers possessing both divinity and academic degrees. Each consequently viewed Carleton as a Christian college, though independent from the Congregational Church that had founded it, functioning, especially after 1900, more as a "historically church-related" institution.

Skinner Memorial Chapel was not dedicated until October 1916, on the occasion of the college's fiftieth anniversary, but Carleton has had a chapel for nearly all of its 150 years. The college's chaplaincy is much younger, not established until 1946, the year Larry Gould, the college's first non-clergy president, appointed Philip Phenix as Carleton's first chaplain. Before the position of chaplain was established, most American colleges typically looked to ordained faculty or cleric presidents to direct the college chapel and to preside over occasions in the life of the institution when the whole community gathered in scholarly convocation or worship. The creation of the chaplain position "gave symbolic expression to the normative religious convictions of the institution and the wider culture."[7]

MAJOR THEMES

Six major themes emerged from this chronological history of the chapel, chaplaincy, and religion at Carleton College.

Student religious and spiritual life was an important component of the educational experience at Carleton since its founding by the Congregational Conference of Minnesota in 1866. In its 150 year history the college has supported student religious life in three ways: a) with a facility, the Willis Chapel before 1916 and the Skinner Memorial Chapel since then, dedicated to community worship and student religious life; b) with college staff, clergy presidents, and faculty before 1945 and chaplains thereafter, to lead, direct, and support student religious life; and c) by providing students with co-curricular programs, organizations, and opportunities.

The college chapel has always served as the college's primary public gathering space, a venue for community worship, official institutional events (convocations, presidential inaugurations), weddings and memorial services, and musical and theater performances. Skinner Memorial Chapel, constructed in 1916, has served Carleton as a church, performing arts center, and auditorium, hosting activities solemn and festive, large and small. Just as the college library served and symbolized the life of the mind, knowledge, and reason, the college chapel served and symbolized the life of the heart, soul, and spirit.

The place of religion at Carleton evolved significantly over the college's 150 years, and can be described by three historical periods. In the tradi-tional Protestant Christian college era (1866–1900) a religious ethos permeated the entire institution and was woven into the mission, the curriculum, and student life. From 1900 to 1965, as American society and colleges became increasingly secular, religion moved from the center to the periphery, out of the curriculum to the co-curriculum, from public to private, and from mandatory to voluntary, with a general decline in student interest and participation. In the third era, since 1970, religion at Carleton has broadened from liberal Protestantism to a multi-faith, multi-form spirituality. Indeed, since 1995 there has been a notable revival of student interest in spiritual life.

Four times in the 20th century the place of religion at Carleton was formally examined, and reports were issued with findings and recommendations: the 1951 Smith Report, the 1959 Barbour Report, the 1964 Religion Requirement Report, and the 1986 Future of the Chaplaincy Report constituted the institution's most extensive and careful examinations of the role of religion and the chaplaincy at Carleton. Although each report suggested the diminishing importance and centrality of religion in the life of the institution, each report also recommended changes to deepen and strengthen the student spiritual experience. Required practice and participation in Protestant services did decrease steadily from 1900 until it was ended in 1964. Yet at each point that traditional religion was diminished, the college intentionally took measures to redefine and address the spiritual needs of students and strengthen the religious program for all students. Indeed, this is a primary thesis of this history of religion and the chaplaincy at Carleton.

Paralleling the diversity and pluralism movements in American society and higher education, the college chaplaincy at Carleton has also changed significantly in the past half century. From 1956 to 1970 David Maitland ministered a traditional (though progressive and liberal) Protestant chaplaincy. From 1970 until his retirement in 1986, Maitland introduced an increasingly more ecumenical, multi-faith, and social justice-oriented approach. In the next decade, Jewelnel Davis redefined the chaplaincy with a pluralistic, multi-formed focus on spirituality and political and social justice. Since 1997 Carolyn Fure-Slocum has expanded and strengthened the contemporary multi-faith, multi-form college chaplaincy, emphasizing meaning-making, interfaith dialogue and social action and encouraging and supporting all students to make spirituality and religion an important, sometimes transformational part of their liberal arts educational experience.

The Carleton chaplaincy and student religious life was significantly shaped by its institutional setting, the distinctively American small residential liberal arts college. Liberal learning at American liberal arts colleges has always been about both the study of the natural world and of the human experience and exploring issues of ultimate meaning.[8] Liberal learning has therefore been about educating both the mind and the heart and soul. The content of that spiritual learning has evolved from Protestant Christianity, to interdenominational, multi-faith and finally to a multi-form spirituality, which Carleton Professor of Religion Bardwell Smith described as

> a concern for the raising of ultimate or religious questions about the nature of man, history, and values. Carleton College as a small liberal arts institution has as its goal

the education of the whole person within a community of persons... within which the various questions about meaning and value are inseparable from the pursuit of knowledge itself and at the heart of which remains the conviction that education involves personal and social responsibility as well as academic excellence.[9]

The liberal arts mission to educate the whole person in the residential setting of community required matters of spirituality, ethics, and social justice to remain an important component of the college mission and the student experience.

Through these six themes, this history chronicles the evolution of the place of religion, the chapel, and the chaplaincy at Carleton College.

Chapter 1

The Nineteenth-Century American Liberal Arts College: The Child of Religion (1866–1900)

CARLETON WAS TYPICAL OF THE Protestant liberal arts colleges founded in the Midwest in the mid- and late-nineteenth century. The early nineteenth-century Protestant denominations believed they were practicing "responsible" Christian democracy by establishing colleges everywhere from New England to the Midwest. The Congregationalists and Presbyterians moved into the upper Midwest and Minnesota, founding Carleton in Northfield and Macalester in St. Paul.[10] Carleton, a Congregational college self-described as a Christian college from its 1866 founding through the 1950s, was established "in the conviction that an institution of learning, distinctly Christian in character, and aiming at the standard of scholarship maintained by the older Colleges of New England"[11] was needed in the new state. The religious nature of early Carleton was implicit in the details of its founding, and explicit in the pages of early college catalogs. The fourth of these, in 1871, declared that the school, "while unsectarian in its aim," was "intended to be emphatically a Christian College." A year later this was expanded into the statement that the institution, though under no ecclesiastical control, took as its purpose "to provide an education liberal and thorough, embracing moral culture as well as mental discipline; and securing a symmetrical Christian character." The 1875 catalog proclaimed the school's intent to be "a true Christian College — not denominational, but distinctly and earnestly evangelical."[12] This statement would remain in the catalog through 1903, when a subtle revision made the language less religious and Christian, striking the phrases "a symmetrical Christian" and "distinctly and earnestly."

The annual reports of Carleton's first president, the Reverend James W. Strong, reflected his view of the centrality and importance of religion in the college's mission, which he believed was built on the twin pillars of reason and faith, liberal learning and religious conviction, empirical knowledge and revelation. Indeed, Strong placed his review of the "Religious Condition of the Institution" at the beginning of his early annual reports, writing in his 1872–73 and 1873–74 annual reports:

> The religious atmosphere of the college has been healthful and stimulating. Prayer meetings have been sustained, not only as formerly on Sabbath afternoon and on Thursday evening, but also each day at noon, and the influence of this daily meeting has been very manifest. Some hopeful cases of conversion have occurred; and so earnest has been the tone of college life, that in no case has there been occasion for unpleasant discipline.[13]

> As to its religious life… No year, since the beginning of this enterprise, has brought us such spiritual blessings. A daily noon prayer meeting was commenced, and in addition to two regular weekly meetings, has continued with an influence for good quite apparent. Soon after the "Day of Fasting and Prayer

The Rev. James W. Strong

for Colleges," special earnestness in prayer and in religious activity was manifested. The whole College was quickened, and as the village pastors engaged in special efforts students were among the first to respond to their appeals to enter at once upon the Christian life. Of our number forty have given the gratifying evidence of a sincere consecration to Christian service… and but one remained in the Ladies' Hall without an expressed hope in Christ. Of the total number enrolled this year, two thirds now claim to be Christians. Such was the religious atmosphere that in March one irreligious parent felt constrained to remove a son and daughter, because, as he said, "it was impossible for them to remain here without becoming Christians." That the revival will have an abiding influence for good upon the College I cannot doubt.[14]

For the next two decades Strong's annual report descriptions of student religious life sounded at times more like that of a proud parish pastor than a college president, though curriculum reform, recruitment (admissions), and fundraising took on steadily increasing importance. Strong seemed particularly pleased when the most evangelical, fervent student believers, always a small number, were most active. He wrote in his 1882–83 report of a "marked development of interest in religious matters… an awakened interest in the welfare of their fellow students... manifest in personal conversations and invitations to the regular meetings in the college, in which eleven or twelve of the young men have publically confessed Christ for the first time."[15] Three years later Strong reported that the religious life of the college had been marked by "uniform activity and notable results," and that

> Never before have we felt so strongly the energy of Christian earnestness and of quiet but aggressive effort on the part of all the students of the institution. The historical noon-day prayer meeting, the meetings of Sunday afternoon and of Wednesday evening were well sustained and indicated a unity of purpose, and a spirit of well-directed Christian Enterprise, that must gladden the hearts of those who see the ends aimed at in the founding of the college, thus fulfilled.[16]

However, by the 1890s Strong's report was primarily devoted to academic and financial concerns, and the religious life report came from the Philosophy Department report and Dean of Women Margaret Evans. For Strong the last two decades of his presidency were devoted increasingly to the small institution's survival, recruiting students, building the faculty, and fundraising. Yet religion maintained a central role to the end of his presidency, and he reaffirmed in his final annual report (1902) his commitment to both scholarship and faith at Carleton:

> Founded as Carleton avowedly was, as a Christian institution to be built up not by State appropriations but by the prayers, the sacrifices, and the gifts of those who felt the need of such a college in Minnesota, of high standards and devout spirit, the twofold aim of thorough scholarship and reli-

Margaret Evans

gious life, has never been forgotten... It was founded to provide... religious training for the spiritual nature. It has seemed to me perfectly plain that Carleton has had no moral right to exist, or to appeal for support, except as an institution caring for the spiritual as well as for the intellectual. In the selection of teachers, my choices have been determined by religious character as well as by intellectual culture. No one has ever been brought into the corps of instructors... unless he was believed to be of earnest Christian character and of high scholarly attainments... It has been my unvarying aim to secure and to retain the very best teachers whom we could command, those combining high scholarship and aptness to teach, with strong personality and devotion to the things.[17]

THE NINETEENTH-CENTURY WILLIS CHAPEL

Willis Hall, the college's first permanent building, served multiple purposes at the infant college. A chapel occupied the first floor; recitation rooms, a meager library, and a science equipment cabinet were on the second floor; the third floor was divided into dormitory rooms for "gentlemen" students; and the basement contained the chemical laboratory.[18] After a fire in 1879 gutted the building, Willis was rebuilt and immediately became, as the 1895 *Algol* (the student yearbook) stated, the "center of our college life,"[19] the focal point for student academic, social, and religious life. It was central to college life for the important activity there:

> The Chapel was placed upon the second floor and made two stories high... In room A Professor Goodhue, the first, last, and only professor of Greek and Dean of the Faculty... in room D Dean Margaret Evans teaches English Literature... in room C are held the noon prayer meeting, the Wednesday evening meetings of the YMCA, and the meetings of the three literary societies... In the Chapel itself all the students assemble each morning for devotional exercises. Here also are the Sunday afternoon prayer meetings, chorus classes, public rhetoricals, and music recitals.[20]

As the campus' largest gathering space, Willis Chapel, like the later Skinner Chapel, hosted not only religious services, but many other college events and music performances.

The chapel in the women's dormitory, Gridley Hall

A small chapel in Gridley, the woman's residence hall, was the scene of Dean Margaret Evans' weekly lecture for the college's young ladies. Evans was a deeply religious educator, and her lectures were informal sermons. One student recalled that Evans' words and presence made a "girl's life seem nobler, more worth the living; which gives higher ideals, and worthier purposes... and teaches us to look with a purer vision into broad fields where our influence may count for true womanhood. It is like a vision to us."[21] The YWCA held many of its prayer meetings and activities in the Gridley Chapel, but all college religious events were held in the Willis Chapel or the nearby Congregational Church.

Student life at Carleton in the late 1800s was consumed by the demanding rigid classic liberal arts curriculum and required participation in religious services and activities.[22] The few social activities

were academic or religious in nature but not required. A coed Student Literary Society was founded in 1869, and literary societies served as the primary student social organization in the nineteenth and early twentieth century. The Philomathian Society, the first permanent group, furnished a reading room in Ladies Hall and held weekly meetings and programs of recitations, readings, debates, essays, and orations. By the 1890s organizations formed for debate and public speaking, dramatic produc-

provided a light, often satirical, portrayal of student life. Overall, strenuous academic work along with pious religious activities characterized the student experience for most Carls, but there was steadily increasing time for social, athletic, and performing arts — and for just having fun. But unlike many colleges where student life was rife with drinking, dancing, pranks, and even violent behavior, at Carleton students generally had fun with appropriate and college-approved activities, so faculty seldom needed to exercise their disciplinary role.

Carleton YMCA members, 1896

Among the student co-curricular enterprises, religious organizations were especially active and influential at nineteenth-century Carleton. As early as 1874, before Carleton had celebrated its first commencement, a coed Students' Christian Association (SCA) was organized "to promote the religious welfare" of students[24] through daily prayer meetings at noon in Willis and weekly meetings Sunday afternoon and Wednesday evenings. In the mid 1880s the SCA split and established Carleton chapters of the Young Men's Christian Association (YMCA) and the Young Women's Christian Association (YWCA). President Strong noted in

tions, and musical performance. The student newspaper, the *Carletonian*,[23] initially created by the Philomathian and Alpha Beta Pi Societies, became the official student newspaper in the 1880s and has published weekly since 1888. The student yearbook (*Algol*) was issued sporadically in the 1890s and

an annual report that the YMCA and YWCA were "vigorously prosecuting the work commonly undertaken by such bodies. Classes for bible studies are held, one daily and three weekly meetings are maintained, and much efficient personal work is done by its members." Throughout the nineteenth century

the YMCA and YWCA offered voluntary opportunities for students to practice and learn about their Christianity.

Dean Margaret Evans summarized the nineteenth-century religious life of Carleton women in her 1901 "Woman's Program" report:

> The religious life of the young women, as is generally the case, has been marked rather by growth and development than by any

special spiritual crises or unusual activity. In a few individual cases the growth and increased spirituality and improvement in life have been unusual; frivolous and careless lives have become entirely changed. The Annual Convention of the YMCA, the Day of Prayer for Colleges, as well as the regular religious exercises and spirit of the college have all proved this year unusually helpful, as was the Geneva Conference attended by three girls. A special impetus to the broadening and deepening of the religious life was given in the winter term by the visit of nine students, four young women and five young men, and a teacher to the Toronto Convention of the Missionary Volunteers. Not only were the religious lives of the delegates stimulated and quickened, but they by their reports, and by the meetings occasioned by them, gave new life to the evangelistic spirit of the entire college. The number of missionary volunteers increased to nine, and in the voluntary Mission Study Class to thirteen young men and women. The returned delegates have done good service, too, in speaking in eight or ten of the churches in neighboring cities and towns. Of the hundred and thirty-seven young women in college this year, all but thirteen are professing Christians.[25]

However, religious life for all Carleton students was defined through the college's religious attendance requirements. The first college catalog proclaimed simply, "All members of the College are required to attend church regularly on the Sabbath." Students were also expected to attend daily devotional exercises, which were by faculty mandate to "be characterized by distinctness of utterance, earnestness of spirit, by brevity without abruptness."[26]

While some students happily embraced the religious activity expectations and most accepted them as appropriate and necessary, a few students found the extensive religion requirements to be excessive, onerous, and not something they wanted in their college educational experience. Students lamented having to study and prepare their lesson while singing and praying at the daily morning devotionals, and when in 1881 the college announced an addi-

The Carleton College campus at the end of the 19th century, showing the future site of the new chapel. Willis Hall is at the left, Gridley Hall at the right.

tional prayer meeting for music students, the student newspaper publically complained: "It would seem that we have enough already."[27] By the 1890s there was considerable discussion of the question of required church attendance, resulting in an 1881 alumnus writing in the *Carletonian*, "May the time come soon when the obnoxious and injurious system of compulsory church attendance shall be abolished at Carleton."

The religious requirements remained into the new century, however, and by 1908, in his final annual report, second president William Henry Sallmon explained that

> The round of religious meetings sustained in the past has not been disturbed, tho *(sic)* there has been a growing conviction that there are too many of them, and that some members of the College community are exposed to religious dissipation... more weight has been given to classes for Bible study than to prayer meetings, which is in accord with the best modern views.[28]

This was the first official expression of an argument and principle that would strengthen and eventually guide the college: students should be required to study religion and address issues of spirituality and meaning, but the practice and exercise of religion should be voluntary. Sallmon also suggested that rather than judging the college's Christian character and life by attendance at required meetings, it should be measured by the "exhibition of honesty, courtesy, and fair-dealing in the classroom, in the literary societies, and upon the athletic field."

When in 1909 Carleton trustees selected a third cleric president, Donald Cowling, with a BA in divinity and a PhD in philosophy from Yale, the intent was to continue and strengthen their vision as an institution of learning, distinctly Christian in character, aimed at the standard of scholarship maintained by the best New England colleges. While clearly not a church-controlled college, Carleton was definitely an institution with the "two-fold aim of thorough scholarship and religious life," where reason and faith, liberal learning and religious conviction, empirical knowledge and revelation were inextricably woven together in a liberal arts education. Although scholarship and the life of the mind were most central and important and increasingly in ascendance, matters of faith, ethics, and spirituality remained an important part of the liberal learning and the student experience. It was not surprising, therefore, that a new chapel was high on the list of needed buildings for the young new president.

Chapter 2

Envisioning, Planning, and Building the Skinner Memorial Chapel
(1909–1916)

I N 1909 DONALD JOHN COWLING WAS appointed Carleton's third president. After earning four degrees — a bachelor and master's in divinity and a master's and doctorate in philosophy — from Yale and teaching philosophy for three years at Baker, a small Methodist college in Kansas, the Reverend Doctor Cowling embarked upon a thirty-six-year presidency at Carleton in which he would recruit a first-rate faculty, strengthen the academic program, realize financial stability with a small but growing endowment, initiate an ambitious facility master plan, and establish Carleton's national reputation as a selective residential liberal arts college with a distinctive Christian character.[29] In his first six years as president Cowling personally envisioned, designed, and oversaw the construction of the building — Skinner Memorial Chapel — that would allow the chapel to continue to serve as the center of campus life and vividly demonstrate and symbolize the continuing importance of religion at the college.

Although Cowling was young and without any academic administrative experience, he was well prepared to lead Carleton. In the May 1910 *Alumni Magazine* alumnus Marion Leroy Burton, who later that year became president of Smith College and subsequently president of the University of Minnesota and then the University of Michigan, introduced Cowling:

> Dr. Cowling fortunately inherited a strong body, the English breadth of view, and a clear conviction of the value of a religious interpretation of life... He is first of all thoroughly human — natural, sane, broad, common-sense, modest. He is a scholar... But above all, President Cowling is a religious man. Both intellectually and practically his

religious convictions are operative. He believes in the thing he is doing. He is convinced that all true education has its religious aspect... In these qualifications it appears that Carleton has in her new President, precisely the things for which she stands in a broad and intelligent way."[30]

As a scholar-cleric, Burton suggested, Cowling was the ideal leader for a Christian liberal arts college and one who would understand the importance of the chapel in the life of the college.

In the same issue of *Alumni Magazine* Cowling announced the "necessity for more building accommodations" with an ambitious list that included a recitation hall, a gymnasium for women, a men's dormitory, a women's dormitory, and a chapel. The need for a new chapel was clear, Cowling wrote to the alumni, as "the present unattractive hall is ill adapted to the religious needs of our students. A suitable building to serve as a center for the religious life of the school would furnish a helpful stimulus to that side of the school's work."[31]

Remarkably Cowling fulfilled that needs list and more. Between 1914 and 1928 he expanded and transformed the college's physical plant and appearance by constructing nine buildings, all by the same Chicago architectural firm of Patton, Holmes, and Flinn, and all in the same collegiate Gothic style. The nine buildings — Music Hall (1914), Skinner Memorial Chapel (1916), the west side men's residence halls [Burton (1915), Davis (1923), and Severance (1928)], the eastern woman's residence halls [Nourse (1917) and Evans (1927)], Leighton Hall of Chemistry (1920), and Laird Stadium (1927) —

were arranged and sited as part of Cowling's grand campus master plan.

President Cowling's intimate, hands-on role in the design, planning, and construction of the new chapel was evident in almost four years of weekly correspondence with Chicago architects Norman Patton, Morris Holmes, and Raymond Flinn. As

Donald J. Cowling

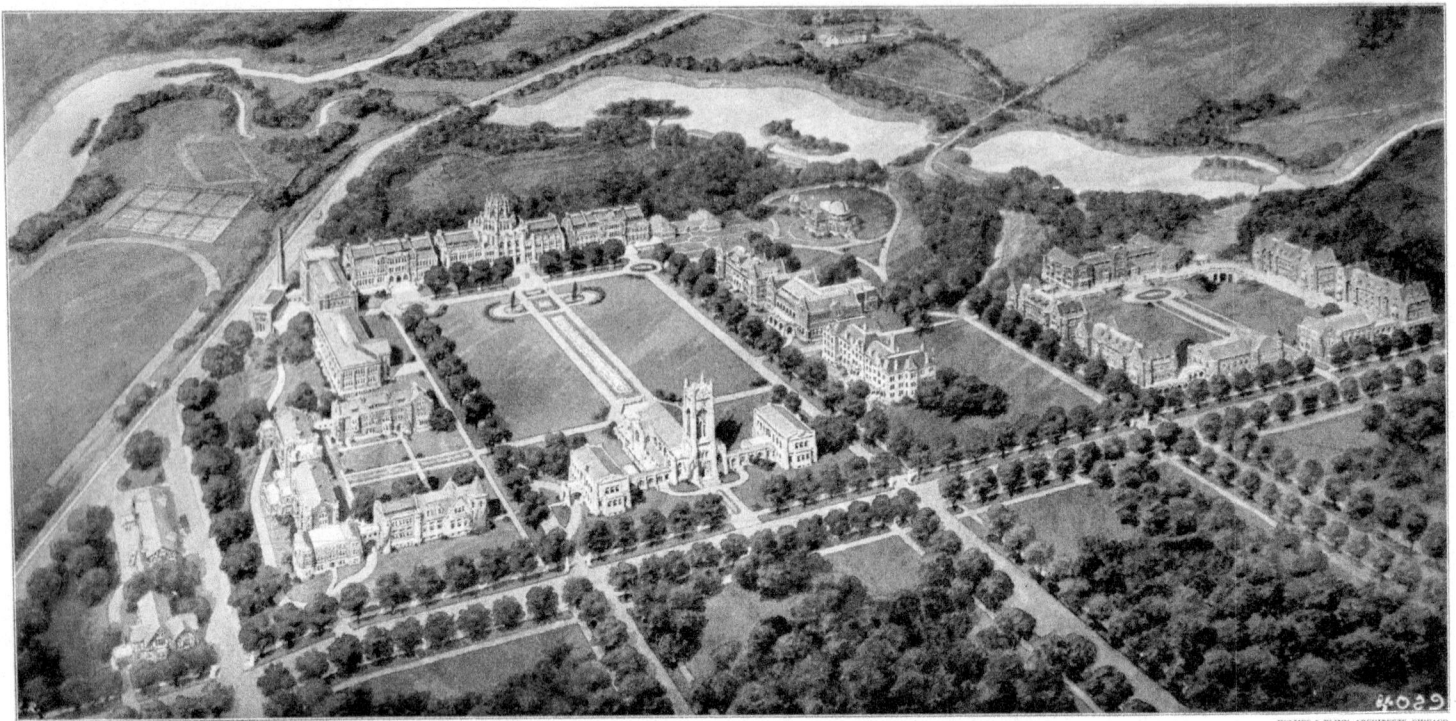

HOLMES & FLINN, ARCHITECTS, CHICAGO

early as January 1912 Patton began work on a campus master plan, which included Item #4 on Cowling's list of building needs: a college chapel with a seating capacity for "at least 800 people" and room for a large chorus and pipe organ to cost not less than $10,000."[32] On the first master plan sketches, Patton placed the chapel, a building of "noble design" on the central axis of the campus to "form an interesting feature" at the south end of campus."[33] The next master plan (September 1913) iteration proposed a "Chapel Group," the chapel with two wings for an administrative and YMCA building, along with the first cost estimates: a chapel, including cloisters, to accommodate 1,000 and a choir of 200 was $90,000; seating for 600 would cost $75,000; and the YMCA and administrative wings were estimated at $25,000 each.

There followed months of discussion and debate between Cowling and the architects about how to make the chapel large and appropriately grand enough, yet affordable. Cowling had a promise from the widow of Northfield merchant and Carleton trustee Miron Skinner to pay up to $75,000 for a chapel. Patton could not design a 1000-seat chapel for that price, unless the tower and vestibules were omitted. But Cowling insisted that the chapel must have a tower.

Looking for other places to reduce costs, Cowling wrote Morris Holmes (who led the project after Patton's sudden death) that he was considering "putting up our new chapel in brick. Brick like was used in the Music building, together with Bedford stone, would unquestionably make a fine appearance. How much cheaper would this be than stone?"[34]

An early chapel sketch with administrative and YMCA wings

Chapter 2

Although stone increased the cost by nearly $6,000, in July 1915 plans were drawn for a stone finished exterior and interior, and a 1200-capacity building with a bell tower. Holmes assured the president that the choice of stone was wise, as the chapel was architecturally the "climax of the whole institution, and (stone) is evidently monumental and quite ap-

propriately of a higher finish," and that the building will "retain its precedence" if it is the one building on campus where highly finished stone was used.[35] Cowling also instructed Holmes to place the main entrance of the chapel facing south toward the town, explaining to the architects that "a great majority of our friends seem to favor facing the chap-

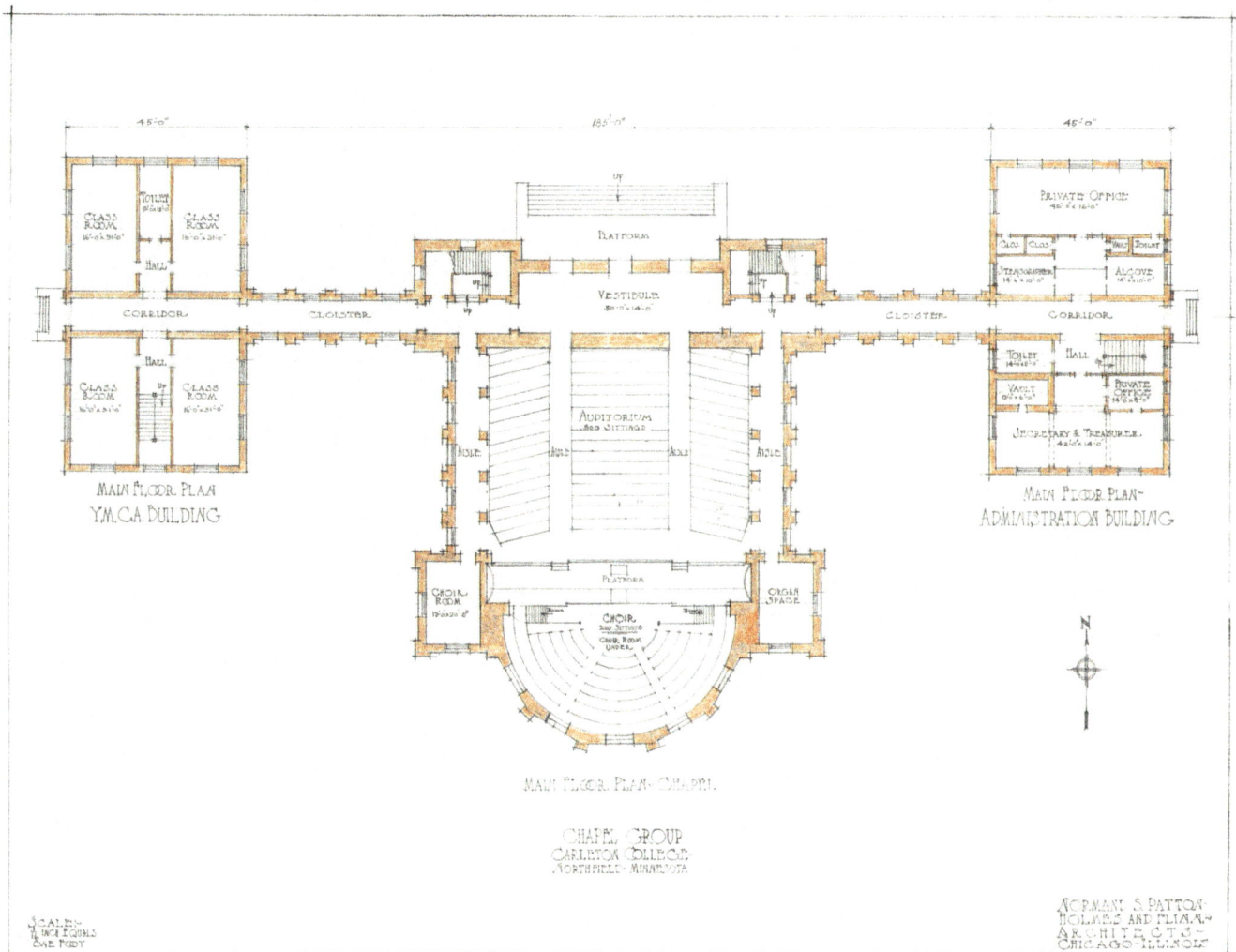

el south toward the street... The woman (Skinner) from who we hope to secure the money also favors very strongly the facing of the chapel toward the street."

In February of 1916 *The Alumni Magazine* reprinted an article from *The Advance* (a publication of the Congregational Church) in which Carleton Professor of Philosophy John Boodin explained that Carleton was "not merely a place" for academic learning and intellectual training, but that the residential liberal arts college was a community where student learning and life needed a "proper moral and religious atmosphere."[36] Founded in faith, Carleton possessed a "spirit of religious loyalty" and a student community with a sound inner life held together by a spiritual bond, a "rugged and wholesome religion" which permeated the college and revealed itself in a common religious devotion, high standards, and the tradition of required chapel.

Boodin continued, "One is impressed with the spirit of solidarity of spirit... that reminds one of Yale more than any western institution. Carleton has always been known for its collective activities... as marked in its religious and literary activities as in its athletics." This religion-based community life had developed and flourished at Carleton despite the "uninviting and uncomfortable" and modest-sized Willis Chapel.

But now, Boodin proudly proclaimed, the "dream of an adequate setting for this collective life" was to be finally realized. The new chapel, he wrote,

> will stand out as one of the finest of its kind in American colleges. In its architecture and by its position it will dominate the college campus and thus form a fitting symbol for the unity of which it is the expression. It will form a suitable home for the rich collective

Miron Skinner, Northfield merchant and Carleton trustee

life which the spiritual traditions of Carleton have already created, and at the same time give them new dignity and meaning.

Boodin also recognized the symbolic importance of the Skinner gift in further strengthening the town-gown relationship. This "bond of interest and cooperation" had been recently enhanced with the co-sponsored Sunday afternoon Community Vesper Service that brought college and community people together to hear some of "the ablest men of the American pulpit." This "new institution," which had "enriched" both community and college in its temporary host in the First Congregational Church, would soon have a "beautiful home" of its own, the Skinner Chapel. This notable college and community program would continue a century later in the Friday morning weekly Carleton Convocations in Skinner Chapel.

A month later, and only six months before the chapel dedication, *The Carletonian* informed the students of the Skinner gift with the headline, "COLLEGE CHAPEL A CERTAINTY / ADDITIONAL GIFT BY MRS. SKINNER MAKES ERECTION POSSIBLE / M. W. SKINNER MEMORIAL":[37]

> The erection in the near future of a $100,000 chapel for Carleton has been made possible by an additional gift of $75,000 from Mrs. M. W. Skinner of Northfield. This new gift together with previous gifts from the Skinner family, will provide for the complete cost of the new structure. The chapel will be a memorial to Miron W. Skinner, a former trustee and faithful supporter of Carleton College.... Miron W. Skinner was ever active in the public affairs of Northfield, and was a member of the board of trustees of Carleton College from its founding until his death. He served on the city council for six years and was mayor for four years. The erection of a chapel on the Carleton campus in memory of Mr. Skinner is significant of the sympathetic and co-operative relations which exist between Carleton College and the people of Northfield. Such a chapel will in the future afford a common meeting place for the townspeople and college folk and so strengthen and preserve the happy relationship which has always existed between them.

Cowling and the architects grappled with a variety of construction issues, including the decorative glass windows, building acoustics, stone crockets on the tower pinnacle, pew selection, and the memorial tablet in the tower vestibule, as he pushed the architects and contractors to complete the chapel for the college's fiftieth anniversary celebration in October 1916. Although Holmes and Flinn served as project superintendent with general contractor Leighton Construction, Cowling personally approved every design decision. Architect Holmes wrote Cowling in

An architects' rendering of the proposed chapel, published in the college's 1915 catalog

Three views of the Skinner Chapel construction in 1915: from the northwest, south, and west.

April 1916 that he had inspected the chapel glass production at the Linden Company to discuss the "motifs" for the decorative panels[38] and confirmed with Cowling a "general understanding that very little ecclesiastical symbolism" was needed and that the chapel glass should be "kept decorative rather than symbolic." The glass motifs that Cowling approved was full of Christian symbolism but had none of the explicit graphic depictions of Christ, the crucifixion, or biblical stories common in church chapels and cathedrals. Apparently the images in the chapel windows, though primarily Christian symbolism, were for Cowling and the architects considered more decorative than ecclesiastical.

When Cowling chose to have the interior of the chapel finished in stone it added, the architects wrote, to the "acoustical problem" inherent in a chapel design driven by "beauty and ecclesiastical significance,"[39] making it necessary to "now let acoustical considerations dominate the choice of materials." To improve the acoustics, natural color burlap covered the ceilings over the rostrum, choir, and gallery (balcony), and the central ceiling was paneled in wood. But the walls remained stone and the floors tile rather than carpet, leaving a building with less than ideal acoustics. The dramatic soaring bell tower was capped with four elaborate stone crockets, decorative spires on the tower's four corners. Though not in the original budget, the architects strongly recommended that the four $100 crockets be added as it would certainly "add to the

beauty of the entire tower."[40] Though seemingly a minor detail, it is difficult now to imagine the chapel tower without the four crockets pointing to the heavens.

Cowling was frustrated by delays with receiving the building stone, the pews, and the memorial tablet. In the summer of 1915, he sent a scolding letter to Holmes that the Indiana-quarried Bedford stone, promised in the spring, had not arrived, leaving Mr. Leighton's construction crew idle and putting the entire project on hold.[41] Not until late October, less than twelve months before the new chapel was to host the college's fiftieth anniversary celebration, did the stone arrive on twenty-seven freight cars, and the walls of the chapel begin to rise from the foundation. Sadly, tragedy struck the construction project six weeks later when a stone worker fell from a scaffold and died of head injuries. In late July 1916, after delays in producing sample pews to test, Cowling directed Holmes to void the pew contract with the Fond du Lac Company and personally made new arrangements with the Minneapolis Office and School Furniture Co., which guaranteed delivery and installation by October 8. In early August Cowling and Leighton made a personal visit to the furniture shop and approved, by sitting on a sample, the shape of the seat and back. The Minneapolis firm had exactly two months to build, deliver, and install the pews; it completed its work the week before the deadline.

Unfortunately, the memorial tablet dedicating the chapel to Miron Skinner was not

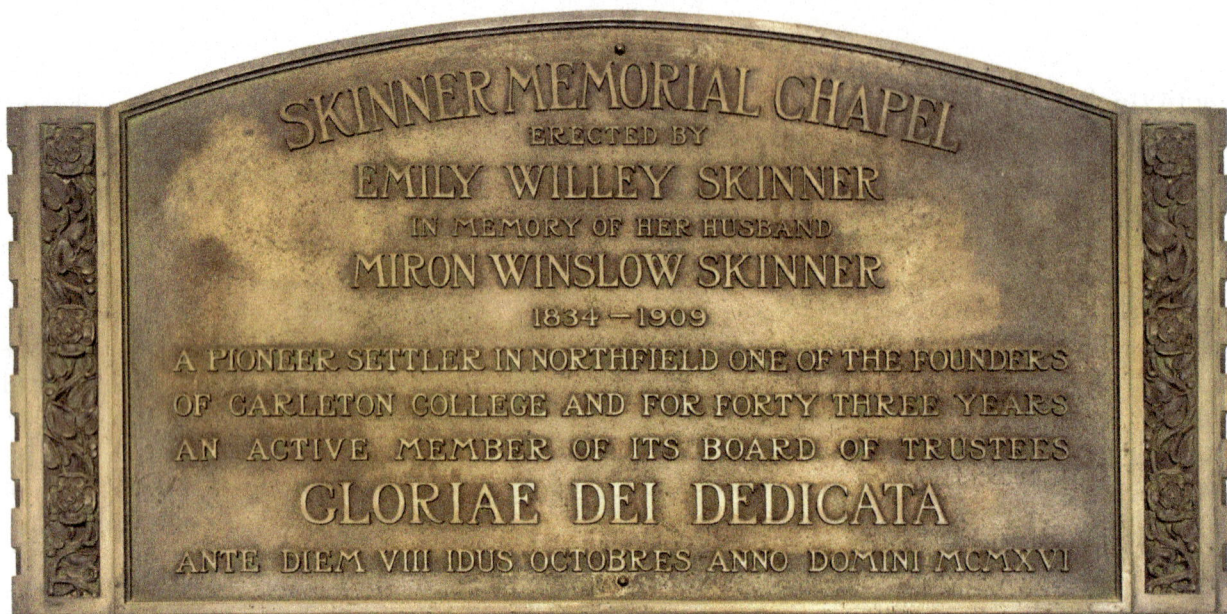

installed in time for the October building dedication. On September 15 Holmes wrote Cowling that the tablet would be made of statuary bronze, the lettering raised and polished and the sunken background dark bronze. However, as he had only then received the inscription from Cowling, he doubted he could have the tablet installed by the October 8 dedication date. Holmes discussed with Cowling the placement of the memorial tablet in the Tower Vestibule; Holmes presented two placements — on the side against the wall or a larger one over the door, recommending the wall placement as "more monumental." Less than three weeks from the dedication, Cowling asked Holmes to ensure that the "curve of the top of the tablet corresponds with the curve of the ceiling," a detail that Mrs. Skinner requested and Cowling was determined to honor. In November the memorial tablet was installed in the south tower vestibule, over the center door to the nave. It read:

SKINNER MEMORIAL CHAPEL
Erected by
Emily Willey Skinner
In Memory of Her Husband
MIRON WINSLOW SKINNER
1834–1909
A Pioneer Settler In Northfield. One of the Founders
Of Carleton College and for Forty-Three Years
An Active Member of the Board of Trustees
Gloriae Dei Dedicata
Ante Diem VIII Indus Octobres Annu Domini
MVMXVI

Cowling was involved in the planning and all of the details of building design and construction, including the careful choice of building materials to ensure his new chapel looked as he believed a college chapel should. For all of the nine buildings constructed in the teens and twenties, Cowling chose an English Late Gothic style, popularly known as collegiate Gothic for its widespread use by American colleges and universities in the late-nineteenth and early-twentieth century. Cowling's choice of a traditional architectural style was hardly surprising, coming from a man who was building his Midwestern college in the image of his alma mater Yale and who said frequently that a college had a responsibility to look like a college. Carleton art historian Lauren Soth explained how the chapel was both similar to and unique among the Gothic Cowling era buildings, noting that the chapel was an exception. Although also based on the English Late Gothic style, the Carleton's stone chapel's model was

> the small parish church, not the great cathedral. It too has strong massing created by a soaring tower, different roof levels, projecting side porches, and transept arms. But it lacks the brick and stone contrast so striking on the other buildings. Its religious significance and central location must have dictated the greater severity of its all-stone exterior.[42]

Cowling's correspondence with the architects confirmed Soth's conjecture that the choice of an

Skinner Memorial Chapel
Dedicated Oct 5th 1916

all-stone exterior and soaring tower was to set the chapel apart, symbolically and visually, from the other campus buildings.

When in 1982 Skinner Memorial Chapel was listed on the National Register of Historic Places, the college provided the Minnesota Historical Society with this architectural description of the chapel:

> Designed in the Late Gothic Revival Style... the building is of reinforced concrete construction faced with random coursed Bedford stone. It has a Latin cross floor plan with a prominent tower at the south end, intersecting transepts, and flanking side aisles. The large square tower is the dominant design element. The main floor tower features include a central transomed doorway in a receding arch with low relief carved tracery and the Carleton shield overhead, and three arched windows above the doorway.
>
> The upper portion of the tower features an open belfry defined with stone tracery, and corner piers topped by finials with crockets, and open balustrade.
>
> Tripartite stained glass windows set in hooded Tudor arches are utilized throughout; engaged buttresses further define the bays and accentuate the corners. Large stained glass windows are centered in the transept and apse ends; transept ends feature stepped coped gables, and the apse end a standard coped gable. A red tile roof with exposed rafter tails covers the main mass of the building.[43]

Except for the memorial tablet, the chapel was ready for its dedication and to host the college's fiftieth anniversary celebration, events of great significance for both the college and Northfield. The dedication of the chapel on Sunday morning, October 8, 1916, opened the college's anniversary week festivities. The *Carletonian* reported that a capacity audience of nearly twelve hundred heard the

FRONT.
CARLETON COLLEGE CHAPEL   MAY 11/14.

Patton, Holmes & Flinn
Architects

11558-J.

Reverend John Gardner, D.D. of the New England Congregational Church of Chicago preach the dedicatory sermon. The choir, "swelled to the number of sixty-eight voices," appeared for the first time in vestments, and the congregation was "charmed" with the music of the great organ which, like the building itself, was the gift of Mrs. Miron Skinner.[44]

After this brief introductory paragraph, the student paper printed the entire text of Dr. Gardner's sermon, "Worship as the Highest Expression of Religion." It was fitting, Gardner suggested, that the fiftieth anniversary celebration should begin with the dedication of "this beautiful House of God," as Carleton's founders realized that the "center of learning" they established was dedicated to helping students "develop their spiritual nature." A new era of Christian higher education was "marked by the erection of this noble edifice whose splendid tower commands the campus and indeed, the whole region." Furthermore, the new chapel was designed to "express and develop the spirit of Carleton," founded upon the recognition that "all true enlightenment comes through an acquaintance with humanity" and that education was founded on the "recognition of the presence and authority and power of God in human life." For President Cowling, Reverend Gardner, and most of the faculty and students, reason and faith formed the foundation of the college, and correspondingly the library and the chapel served as the centers of campus life.

The *Northfield News* provided a different perspective of the anniversary celebration and the building dedication. The front-page article headlined "Historic Week for Carleton" highlighted the Monday evening Dedication of the Organ ceremony, proclaiming that "With more than fifteen hundred people packed into spacious Skinner Memorial

Professor Gillette at the new chapel organ

Chapel the dedication of the magnificent new organ was the outstanding event in public interest of the opening days of Carleton's anniversary week."[45] While the Sunday morning chapel dedication service was a distinctly Carleton event, the organ dedication was a college *and* community occasion. President Cowling announced that the $22,000 pipe organ, built by the J. W. Steere & Son Organ Company of Springfield, Massachusetts, was the gift of Northfielder Mrs. M. R. Skinner, "whose generosity and love for the college," the *News* reminded its readers, "had already been expressed in the gift of the new chapel." The Carleton trustees acknowledged the gift by designating the instrument the Emily Willey Skinner Organ. Following the formal announcement of the gift and a prayer of dedication from Northfield's Reverend E. B. Dean, nationally renowned organist W. Lynnwood Farnum of the Emmanuel Church Boston played a program that "brought out the varied and wonderful tones of the instrument" and although the musical selections may have been too "classic" for many of the townspeople, "all appreciated what it means to have such a splendid instrument in Northfield."

The new chapel, and especially the soaring 108-foot bell tower, were universally praised and became an immediate campus landmark. The new chapel was undoubtedly the most imposing building in Northfield, as its tower reached a height visible from all of the surrounding country. *The Carletonian* suggested that the chapel tower "built as it is of the white Bedford Stone would be a striking and artistic advertisement of Carleton if it were properly illuminated at night."[46] President Cowling wrote architect Raymond Flinn that "The satisfaction of the hundreds of people who were here last week with the chapel is simply wonderful. I do not believe I ever heard a building given such unquali-

fied praise."[47] Carleton professor Charles Mierow claimed that the Carleton Chapel was an example of the typical American college chapel, "suited not only to strictly religious services but to other formal and dignified academic occasions."[48]

The Skinner Chapel was prominently featured in many college publications. The inside cover photo in the January 1919 alumni magazine, an image of the chapel in winter, was captioned with the Wordsworth quote "Spires whose 'silent finger points to heaven.'" In the December 1919 issue of the magazine, Carleton professor Ambrose White Vernon wrote of the significance and power of the chapel:

> That building expresses more than faith in God. It expresses faith in Carleton and Minnesota, and in the eternal relation of beauty to Carleton and Minnesota. That building builds the future. It is difficult to recollect any pile of stone and mortar that is so alive as the Skinner Chapel. It is even more of a creator than it is of a creation. It adds to every sermon and oratorio that is given in it. It is the mute but immutable judge of all the campus; it is the unseen moulder of all the other buildings. It is, perhaps, the best member of the faculty, for it outlasts them all; perhaps it is more lucid and suggestive than any of them.[49]

Although White's words may seem exaggerated and overblown now, they aptly captured the important place religion and the new chapel held for Cowling and the college community.

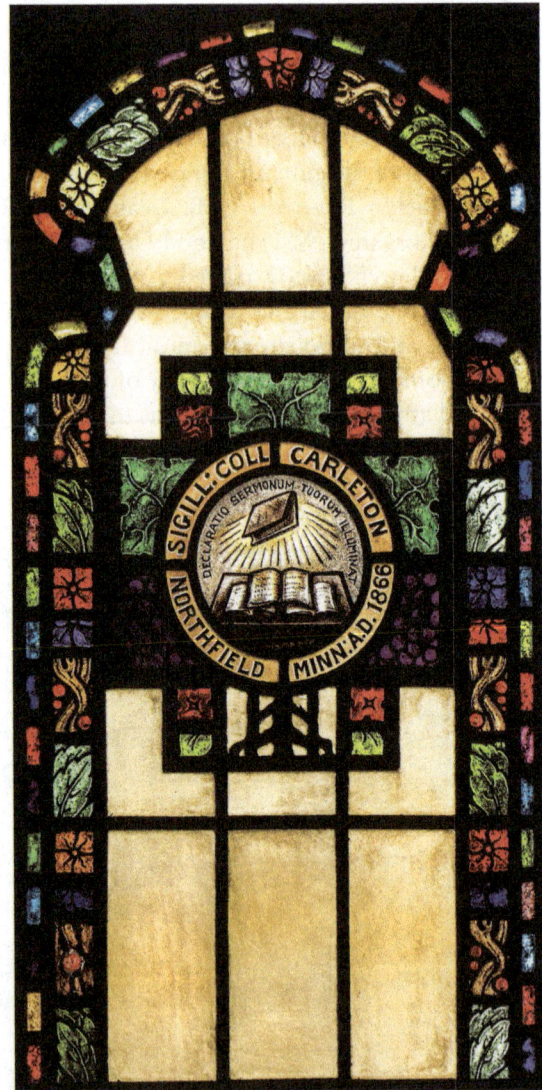

CARLETON COLLEGE
News Bulletin

PVBLISHED MONTHLY DUR-
ING THE COLLEGE YEAR AT
NORTHFIELD MINNESOTA

FEBRUARY 1921

VOLUME THREE   NUMBER FIVE

Chapter 3

The Chapel and Religious Life during the Cowling Presidency (1916–1945)

J ust as President Cowling envisioned and personally oversaw the design and construction of the Skinner Chapel, throughout his thirty-six-year tenure he guided and shaped the religion program and defined the place of religion at the college. Cowling led Carleton as both an academic and religious leader, serving as president and pastor to the college community. Consequently, Carleton would not establish the chaplain position until the appointment of Larry Gould, its first non-cleric president, in 1945. In an address early in his presidency titled "The Small College," Cowling wrote, "There is a real place in the need of the country for the small Christian College. By the Christian College I mean the denominational college, and in these there is an effort to make the atmosphere of the college and the training distinctly Christian."

In 1911 Board of Trustees president David Jones wrote that Carleton stood for both scholastic achievement and high standards, a broad and practical culture that prepared graduates for "intelligent service and useful citizenship." Yet he emphasized that

> the spirit of our College is Christian in its very best sense: not narrow, not sectarian. An atmosphere is found at Carleton in which manly and womanly virtues can be easily propagated. The religious influences about the students there are quietly impressive, and never strained. Is not such a place the finest environment for young men and women during their formative years in college?[50]

Carleton and church relations. Cowling, ordained in the United Brethren Church, assumed a new denominational affiliation with the Carleton

presidency and launched a significant career in Congregationalism. Returning to his Yale training, Cowling wrote

> The influence of Congregationalism is an influence in behalf of freedom of opinion, of liberty of conscience, creedal statements consistent with facts, democracy, and brotherhood, and above all a personal relationship with God, the obligations of which are understood in terms of social justice and moral righteousness, and not in terms of theological demands nor the sanctions of ecclesiastical authority.[51]

This liberal progressive Congregationalism provided an ideal rationale for strengthening academic life in a Christian context and for the nonsectarian liberal arts college to reject religious fundamentalism and church authority. Carleton under Cowling was an institution influenced, though not controlled, by its Congregational heritage.

Cowling became a state and national leader in both religion and education: he served as president of the Minnesota Home Missionary Society and the Board of the Congregational Conference of Minnesota as well as being a leader with the Association of American Colleges, the Carnegie Foundation, and the American Council on Education. This was a natural external leadership role for Cowling, Carleton president and preacher. Indeed, Carleton's influence from national church organizations expanded under Cowling, with new cooperative relationships with the Northern Baptist Church (established in 1920 with a $220,000 gift to the college) and the Episcopal Church in Minnesota (1923). Although none of the national church organizations exercised any formal authority over the college, they influenced the college through the close relationship with its clergy president, and by providing Board of Trustees members, speakers for Sunday services, vespers, and chapel, and prospective students. The college also cooperated with the three national organizations by 1) inviting denominational representatives to speak at chapel and hold conferences with student groups; 2) providing its facilities for conferences and institutes, including the national Congregational summer youth conference, the Episcopal Summer Conference for Church Workers, and the summer Minnesota Baptist Conference; 3) sponsoring the

"Annual Carleton Sunday" when Carleton faculty preached in area churches; and 4) having a minister from each of the three local churches sit on the Carleton faculty Committee on Religious Activities.

Yet Cowling's ecumenical approach of affiliation with three denominations proved to be problematic. A theological liberal, Cowling believed that sectarian division hampered the social and evangelical work of Christianity. It was the opportunity to advance denominational unity and expand Carleton's base of potential students that motivated Cowling to engineer the cooperative arrangements with the Minnesota Baptists and Episcopalians. Under these agreements, the two denominations, neither of which had its own college in the state at the time, "adopted" Carleton as their respective church school. Members of each denomination sat on the Carleton Board of Trustees, each denomination's preparatory schools pointed their students toward Carleton, and each denomination pledged small amounts of money to the college. In return, members of the Carleton board were invited to sit on the boards of Baptist and Episcopalian preparatory schools, the college offered its campus for denominational conferences during the summers, and President Cowling helped the denominations raise funds for general education programs.

In 1926 this Christian cooperation hit a formidable rock in the form of Rev. William Bell Riley, the conservative pastor of the First Baptist Church of Minneapolis.[52] Riley was founder and leader of the World Christian Fundamentals Association — best known for having recruited William Jennings Bryan to assist the prosecution in the Scopes Trial — and labeled by Bryan himself as "the greatest statesman of the American pulpit." Riley, in the midst of a campaign to pass an "anti-evolution" bill in Minnesota,

discovered that Carleton was itself harboring evolutionists and other "modernists." He excoriated the college for being "rankly liberal, with a tendency to Unitarianism," and standing "for nothing but the right to indulge in skepticism." Riley demanded that the Minnesota Baptist Convention sever its ties to Carleton because "it is known that practically the entire faculty hold to and teach the evolutionary hypothesis, generally conceded to be anti-Biblical...." The Convention appointed an investigative committee which reported in 1928 that Carleton was an eminently Christian school. But Riley's point was that it was not a *fundamentalist* school, and that year the Convention narrowly agreed to disassociate from Carleton. The more liberal parent Northern (later American) Baptist Conference, the Congregational Church, and the Episcopal diocese of Minnesota continued to consider Carleton a church college, however. For their part, the Carleton faculty thanked President Cowling for preserving their academic freedom.

The college's fiftieth catalog,[53] published the year after the Skinner Chapel was dedicated, illustrated vividly the place of religion at Carleton. Following a listing of the board, faculty, and administrative officers the section "College Preachers" recorded the speakers at the required Sunday morning or Sunday evening vespers service. Of the thirty-six college preachers listed, five were Carleton faculty (Cowling, Fred Hill, A. E. Vestling, Walter Patton, and John Boodin), three were preacher presidents from other Midwest liberal arts colleges (Beloit, Grinnell, and Hamline), three were divinity school deans or faculty, and the remainder were ministers from Protestant congregations throughout the East and Midwest.

The schedule of the "Fiftieth Anniversary Exercises" suggested a celebration worthy of a true church-run college.[54] The first four days of the week-long celebration were entirely devoted to religion. Sunday featured the Reverend Gardner's sermon at the morning Skinner Chapel dedication service and an address at the late afternoon Community Vesper Service. Monday a supper "under the auspices" of the Minnesota Congregational Club preceded the evening dedication of the Emily Willey Skinner Memorial Organ. Sessions of the Minnesota Congregational Conference were held Tuesday and Wednesday. An educational conference under the Conference of the Colleges of the Interior opened with an address by Chicago Theological Seminary President Ozora Davis titled "The Historic Relation of the Church and the College." The session's general topic was "The College and the Religious Life of Students."

Only later in the day did the focus turn from religion to liberal arts education, with a series of afternoon "greetings" from the presidents of Hamline, Macalester, St. Thomas, Gustavus Adolphus, St. Olaf, Knox, and Beloit, and evening addresses from the presidents of Oberlin, Mount Holyoke, and the University of Minnesota. Although the coincidental opening of a grand college chapel undoubtedly added to the religious emphasis of the college's fiftieth anniversary exercises, the week's schedule more so reflected Cowling's belief of the centrality and importance of religion in his residential liberal arts college. The anniversary week concluded on Friday with a more traditional education-focused

program: a morning academic procession into the chapel to hear addresses from Presidents Burton of Smith College, Slocum of Colorado, and Lowell of Harvard, a Phi Beta Kappa Luncheon, an afternoon Alumni Association meeting, an inspection of the new buildings, the Carleton-Macalester football game, and an anniversary dinner with a program of after-dinner speeches which included the presidents of Lake Forest, Oberlin, and Pomona Colleges, retired Carleton Dean Margaret Huntington Evans, and the governor of Minnesota.

The college's statement of "Purpose" in its fiftieth year, as it dedicated the Skinner Chapel, summarized Cowling's belief of the place of religion in his liberal arts college:

> The College aims to provide for its students a broad and liberal culture... for those who desire a full four-year college course as a foundation for later professional study and life work. The College is especially concerned with the moral welfare of its students. It strives to preserve a genuine Christian atmosphere and to have all of its influences count for the development of strong and well-grounded character.[55]

Fourteen years later, in 1930, the college had the same statement of purpose, word for word. By 1940, five years from the end of Cowling's thirty-six-year presidency, the Purpose statement continued to emphasize the place of religion in the life of the college:

> From the founding of the College those responsible for its management have definitely planned to surround its students with a religious atmosphere, provide for them favorable conditions for personal religious development, and to offer opportunities through curriculum and otherwise for understanding the meaning and importance of religion. Although academic work in religion is not required, a wide variety of courses are offered in the literature of the bible, the philosophy and history of religion, Christian thought, and ethics.... Carleton aims throughout its entire teaching program to represent a point of view and a spirit which will contribute to the moral and religious development of its students and to their training for effective service to society.[56]

Within Cowling's long presidency, Carleton had evolved from an institution where all were expected to study and practice the Christian religion to a college concerned with the "moral and religious development" of its students. As the American college (and society) grew more secular and strengthened its academic mission, this ethical and moral development of students, often referred to as "Christian character," was seen as the primary reason for the church and religion to remain in the business of education, especially at nonsectarian residential liberal arts colleges like Carleton.

Macalester College, a Presbyterian residential liberal arts college in St. Paul, was on a similar path with its evolution from a nineteenth-century frontier Christian academy to a twentieth-century selective residential liberal arts college. In the 1920s Macalester President John Carey Acheson, a liberal Protestant like Cowling who was also strengthening the college's academic and intellectual life, argued that Macalester's religious and church role should be focused on and limited to the development of students' Christian character. Acheson suggested that a new emphasis on character building would require a new college position of campus minister to attend to the religious life of the campus and the pastoral needs of students[57] and recommended establishing a college chaplain position. However, no such conversations occurred at Carleton during the Cowling presidency. Cowling saw no need for a chaplaincy as he believed he and the faculty were providing adequate campus ministry.

The faculty role in the Christian college. Like his predecessors, President Cowling believed the faculty were the key to strengthening the college, and he endeavored to "improve" the faculty by finding men who were "at once thoroughly grounded in the matter of personal character and capable and well trained in their special field."[58] In his first decade, he added faculty with PhDs from the best Eastern universities who also believed in the purpose and ideals of Christian education. With retirements and new faculty positions, Cowling wrote that he had the "opportunity to bring together a group of strong men professionally who at the same time believe in the ideals of a distinctly Christian college."[59] Cowling, like other college preacher presidents of the time, enlisted the support of faculty, especially those ordained in one of the Protestant denominations, to share the pastoral tasks of delivering sermons and advising students.

In the person of Professor of Biblical Literature Fred B. Hill, Carleton class of 1900, Yale PhD, and ordained Congregational minister, Cowling found everything he sought in a faculty member for his Christian college. Hill was a superb classroom teacher, and his courses on the social gospel were challenging and inspirational. In one especially popular course, "The Social Teaching of Jesus and Modern Social Problems," Hill's Protestant liberalism sometimes sparked the ire of the more traditional orthodox students.[60] Yet Hill made his greatest impact on the spiritual and social lives of students, and demonstrated the power and influence that a faculty/staff religious leader, even one without a formal role or title, can have at a small residential liberal arts college. In December 1910 Hill offered bible study sessions in his home, and seventy-five men signed up. Hill advised the campus YMCA, leading a group at the annual regional conference in Lake Geneva. His individual advising with Carleton men and women was legendary. Hill served as an unofficial dean of students and chaplain decades before those positions were established at Carleton.

Tragically, in January 1919 Hill died of influenza, caught at age forty during a humanitarian tour of post-war Europe. The stunned campus community mourned the loss of one of its best-loved and most influential teachers. The entire issue of the February 1919 *News Bulletin*, the alumni magazine, was dedicated to Hill.

In his memorial service eulogy in the packed Skinner Chapel, Cowling praised Hill's special impact on Carleton students: "As a friend and counselor to young men and women, he had no equal; his aptitude for reaching them was nothing short of genius...."[61]

Senior Phillip F. Sherman, representing the students, spoke of Hill's masterful teaching, support of athletics, and community service, but he thought it most significant that Hill "stood for the best in religious life":

> He preached, and lived the kind of Christianity that appeals to College men and women, emphasizing the practical and social importance of the church, and showing how to apply Christian principles to our student problems...

What endeared him to us... was the personal touch. Who will ever forget the cheery smile of greeting which he had for everyone? He wanted to know us, to be close to us all. Some of us will never forget the evenings spent in his home... The ever-willing counsel he gave to the Christian Associations... The difficulties of every kind in solving in which he has been a help are beyond number.

Let us stand for the best in everything, let us be steadfast for the right against the wrong, let us live to serve others, as he did. Only by doing so can we honor the memory of Professor Hill.[62]

Sherman's classmate J. Arthur Hughes wrote "A Student's Appreciation" in the same alumni magazine, confirming Cowling's praise for Hill's "genius" for reaching students:

The death of Professor Hill has left an ache in many a student's heart. His was a noble, generous, altruistic spirit, and with his passing something has gone out of our life.

To many he was an intimate personal friend. A man of wealth and high social standing, and in an official position which made him seem somewhat inaccessible from the student's viewpoint, Fred B. Hill's democratic spirit and genial personality made acquaintance inevitable. In him, the student found a man who had the student point of view, and whose primary interest was in student problems.... His death meant the removal of a real friend, one of those friends whose counsel is sound and always to be had for the asking....

He was deeply interested in the moulding of student aims and student ideals. To this end he encouraged informal groups to meet him in his home to discuss student problems....

He was beloved of all who knew him in this intimate way, and there was much of comradeship and nothing of disrespect in the habit of speaking of him as "Freddie B." His was the connecting link between student and faculty. He crystallized Carleton's ideals, and helped us view things as he did.... As class dean he wielded a most potent influence for high college standards.

To many the passing of Fred B. Hill marks the passing of an intimate and inspiring friendship. To many more it signifies the departure of a generous, democratic spirit, of a Christian manliness in the largest significance of these terms. To us, the students of Carleton College, it means the passing of a type of man indispensable to the small college; it means the passing of a leader.[63]

Fred Hill, along with Bardwell Smith later in the twentieth century, were two of the most important Carleton faculty in the spiritual lives of Carleton students.

The Faculty Committee on Religious Activities (CRA). This faculty committee, working closely with the president (and occasionally with the Carleton Student Association's Chapel Committee) planned, directed, and guided the college's required religious activities, functioning as the predecessor to the future Office of the Chaplain. The Religious Activities Committee's reports during the Cowling era show they were concerned with the operation and quality of the daily chapel exercises, as well as the Sunday evening vespers and the Sunday morning service. Faculty also advised the student religious groups, primarily the YMCA and YWCA. Many faculty in the early-twentieth century felt a responsibility for the moral education of their students, an obligation especially keen at small residential liberal arts colleges like Carleton. This work occurred primarily outside of the classroom, as the 1928 CRA Report[64] noted that "The committee will continue its efforts to interest faculty members in the religious and moral welfare of students.... A number of instructors sought contacts with students for this purpose, either visiting them in their rooms or inviting them to faculty homes." Periodically the CRA sponsored discussions led by President Cowling "regarding the place of Religion in modern life and in the Christian College" that usually proved to be "stimulating and profitable."

By the end of the Cowling presidency the CRA was meeting infrequently but still overseeing, with the president, the evolving campus religious life and activities. The 1942–43 CRA Report noted that the once daily chapel was now only Tuesday mornings, and the "strictly devotional" service consisted of readings, prayers, and music. Additional convocations were frequently held during the week, but it was a "definite policy" not to let anything interfere with the Tuesday devotional period.[65] The Sunday evening vesper service continued to occupy the central place on the religious program of the college.

In 1914 Cowling and the CRA established a Sunday afternoon Community Vespers Program, held in the nearby Congregational Church. With the goal of bringing to the students the "very strongest preachers in the country," Cowling made the weekly sermon and lecture series one of his "hobbies" for the year and soon deemed it a "first-rate success," as it drew 600 to 700 townspeople, faculty, and students each Sunday. Yet the necessity of holding this innovative, high-profile community event off-campus highlighted the lack of a college facility able to accommodate sizable audiences and motivated Cowl-

ing to initiate a building campaign that produced the 1200-capacity chapel two years later.[66] Skinner Chapel, with its front doors open to the town, was the ideal venue for the Community Vespers and it has hosted a weekly community lecture program, known after 1970 as the Friday morning Carleton Convocation, for a century now.

Required religious participation. The 1916–17 catalog confirmed the religious activity required for students, as it had been for their nineteenth-century predecessors:

> A chapel service, conducted by members of the faculty, is held daily and not only maintains the religious traditions of the College, but also unites the student body once each day, thus giving the College a spirit of unity otherwise impossible. A community Vespers service each Sunday afternoon with many speakers of national reputation.... Attendance: Students are required to attend regularly the classes in which they are enrolled, chapel exercises on each school day, and at least one service of public worship each Sunday.[67]

With the Skinner Chapel's opening in 1916, all campus religious activities could now be accommodated on campus. The primary components were these: daily morning chapel exercises; Sunday morning Protestant service; and the Sunday afternoon or evening Vespers service. Students were required to attend every day, though by the early 1920s with the enrollment growing, the requirement became three times per week: upperclassmen on Tuesdays and Thursdays, freshmen on Monday and Wednesdays; everyone on Friday. But for all the required chapel exercises, Professor O. C. Helming, chair of the Faculty Committee on Religious Activities (CRA) wrote in his 1926–27 report, "Great care was to be exercised in the arrangement of the services and the appointment of speakers and provision of good music. The exercises were planned with a view to creating a genuinely religious atmosphere."[68]

However, by 1931, fifteen years after Skinner Chapel was built, the formal chapel services for students had been reduced from three times weekly to twice a week and the Sunday evening vespers had become the college's primary religious service. President Cowling had designed vespers in his vision of a Christian college, a service led by clergy and highlighted by sermons from himself, Carleton faculty, and nationally acclaimed clergy, often academics at divinity schools or ministers from top Congregational churches. Vespers brought religion and liberal culture together with liberal intellectual Protestant sermons.

Many Carleton students of course did not share Cowling's vision of the Christian college and complained about the religious attendance requirements or the quality of the many chapel services and activities. Cowling and the faculty increasingly involved students in the planning of the official religious activities and appealed to students to take the required chapel seriously. Most students apparently did so, although many privately complained or poked fun at the college's religious requirements. The 1936 *Algol* suggested launching a campaign for reform that included an "ice cream stand in the vestibule of the Chapel, Pullman accommodations for Vespers, two reel comedies during week day chapel with uniformed nurses to read subtitles to the Freshman, and to allow seniors who want to attend Chapel to meet in the Little Theater, or stay at home."[69]

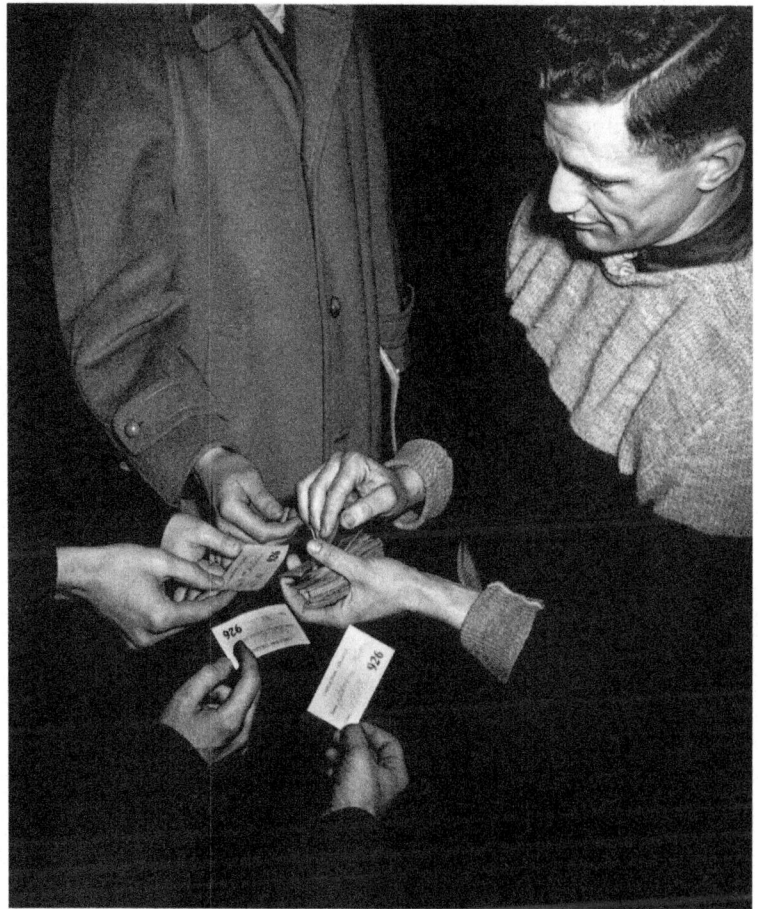

Submitting chapel attendance vouchers, 1940

Student religious organizations. While the president and faculty provided the formal religious activity — academic courses on the Bible, required Sunday morning service, Sunday afternoon vespers, and weekday devotional chapel — it was in the student Christian organizations, the Young Men's Christian Association (YMCA) and the Young Women's Christian Association (YWCA), that student religious life was centered.

The 1915 student yearbook, the *Algol*, claimed that since 1885 the "religious life of the college men has centered about the Y.M.C.A.,"[70] whose prime purpose was to "systematize" student religious activities and "bind together into a common democracy all the men of Carleton." The work of the association was pervasive: new student orientation, mailing a student handbook to prospective freshmen, the social "breaking-in" joint reception at Gridley, and throughout the year "violent outcroppings of religio-social spirit" in get-togethers, rallies, pow-wows, and carnivals that made the YMCA appear to be the "most uproarious organization in the college." But the real work of the association was to be found in the Wednesday evening prayer meeting where "problems of everyday life were threshed out" in Bible study gatherings designed to "tie down more definitely the life of the college man to the principles of Christianity" and in social service activities, leading local Boy Scout patrols, or teaching Sunday School classes in town. Through these activities, formal and informal, religious and social, the YMCA exercised a "constant influence on student life throughout the week."

The YWCA claimed to have the same influence on the lives of Carleton women, taking credit on their 1915 *Algol* page for Carleton's statewide reputation as a college with a "high moral and religious standard" and a "clean and wholesome" atmosphere. Like the men, Carleton's Christian women viewed their association as democratic, open, and inclusive, proudly proclaiming the YWCA was the one organization in the school "to which any girl may belong." Some YWCA activities were similar to the men's, sponsoring new student activities, socials, and Wednesday devotional meetings, but others were for women only — a Christmas sale, girls track meet, and the May fete festival. Carleton women also had the the

Homecoming, 1923

The Little Chapel c. 1955 with Chaplain David Stowe (see page 60)

Gridley Chapel and parlor to hold smaller religious services and meetings.

While the Skinner Chapel served its primary purpose — to provide a place for the entire campus community to worship and gather for college lectures and musical events — admirably, it was too large and impersonal for smaller religious gatherings. In January 1934 a group of students received permission to hold a Wednesday morning pre-breakfast service in a small vacant storage room in the Skinner basement. Thus the idea for a new "little chapel" was conceived.

The October 10, 1934 *Carletonian* announced the opening of a small "medieval" chapel "where students of any communion of the Christian church may meet for religious services."[71] The original unpainted brick wall and cement floor room had been transformed into a place with a medieval old-world atmosphere, with a dark stained-oak alter and railing, cross, candlestick, and embroidered curtain that made an "appropriately rich" background for small group or solitary worship. A small "beautifully-toned" pipe organ had been transferred from the College Music Hall. The Little Chapel (known as the "Crypt" in the late 20th century) has ever since served as a worship venue for Carleton Christian groups and individuals, especially Catholic and Episcopalian students.

Both the men's and women's Christian Associations supported off-campus service work. Every summer thirty to fifty Carleton students attended the YMCA/YWCA Lake Geneva Conference, joining 600 students from Middle West colleges to learn about bible study, mission work, and other "phases of Christian activity." The 1917 *Algol* extolled the significance of the Geneva Conference experience as one of the "great opportunities" of college life, unique as it "deals so directly with those issues of life which are most fundamental in education," purpose and service to others. Both Christian organizations also supported the Congregational Church's Home and Foreign Mission activities and the Carleton Mission in China program which was most active during the Cowling presidency. This missionary desire to serve others, in the local community, the nation, and overseas, has been present throughout Carleton's history, and Carleton students' Christian mission work was the predecessor for the college's service and international programs later in the twentieth century.

In 1943 the President's Office authored a "Statement Regarding Religious Interests and Activities at Carleton,"[72] a twenty-item list of the "definite steps which the College has taken to emphasize the importance of religion in the life of the College and to strengthen its relations with the cooperating denominations." Created to reassure the Congregational, Northern Baptist, and Episcopal Churches that they "remain today as helpful and influential in the life of the College as they have ever been," the statement obscured the reality of the fading influence of a relationship with the churches that was never particularly strong or significant. However, the statement did summarize the Christian legacy that Cowling hoped to leave for his successor. The first two items summarized the college's Christian heritage — its founding as a "Christian College" in 1866 by

a board appointed by the Minnesota Conference of Congregational Churches with church-going faculty who were "in sympathy with religion." Indeed, it listed ten current faculty members (including the president) who were ordained ministers. The catalog's annual Statement of Aims was repeated:

> From the founding of the College those responsible for its management have definitely planned to surround its students with a religious atmosphere, provide for them favorable conditions for personal religious development, and to offer opportunities through curriculum and otherwise for understanding the meaning and importance of religion.

Yet the next ten items described various college activities with the national denominations, most of modest significance for college life: issuing invitations to speak at chapel, offering its facilities for conferences and institutes, encouraging students to enter the ministry, conducting pulpit exchanges, and organizing monthly "local church nights" on campus. The three denominations were included on the Faculty Committee on Religious Activities and often had a representative on the Board of Trustees. Overall, however, the relationship of the three national denominations with the college was superficial and fading. The college was redefining for itself what it meant to be a Christian college. This process would accelerate when two years later, in 1945, Carleton replaced the retiring Cowling with Professor of Geology Laurence Gould, Carleton's fourth president and first non-cleric leader.

Chapter 4

The Chapel, Chaplaincy, and Religious Life in the Gould Presidency (1945–1962)

UPON DONALD COWLING'S RETIREMENT IN 1945, Laurence Gould, Carleton professor of geology and famed Antarctic explorer, became Carleton's fourth, and first non-cleric, president. Gould attended weekly services at the local Episcopal Church and Sunday vespers in Skinner Chapel. The new president inherited an institutional statement on religion that proclaimed that the college from its founding had planned to "surround its students with a religious atmosphere... and to offer opportunities... for understanding the meaning and importance of religion."[73] Although no academic work in religion was required for graduation, Carleton aimed "throughout its entire teaching program to represent a point of view and a spirit which will contribute to the moral and religious development of its students." While the practice of liberal Congregationalism through devotional services had been reduced, maintaining a Christian environment and student moral and religious development continued as important components of the college's purpose and program. Gould understood that while twentieth-century American society was increasingly secular, the spiritual needs of students had not diminished: "It seems to me that while man belongs to the changing world of events, even more so does he belong to an eternal world of the spirit."[74] Thus religion would have an important, though different, place in the Gould era at Carleton.

The 1946 catalog's description of campus "Religious Activities" portrayed a postwar campus religious landscape similar to that late in the Cowling years: a Sunday morning chapel service; a vesper service each Sunday evening with music furnished by the Chapel Choir and nationally notable outside speakers; a brief chapel service, usually conducted by the president, each Tuesday morning at ten o'clock, and a second all-college assembly each Friday morning. Attendance at one of the Sunday services and both of the brief Tuesday and Friday sessions was required. The catalog listing of the speakers at the Sunday evening vespers, previously called "Sermons" and now titled "Public Occasions," reflected the variety of non-religious topics covered: less than a third of the 1946 vesper services were religious sermons, the majority now consisting of music recitals and concerts, illustrated lectures, and convocation addresses. The Carleton Mission in China and the YWCA were the only two active student religious organizations, as the YMCA had gone inactive when the men went off to war. The religious activities section concluded with information about the three local churches with whom the college now had an established relationship, the Congregational-Baptist, the Episcopal, and the Methodist Church.

Laurence Gould opens the Chapel doors for his inauguration, 1945

Philip Phenix: Carleton's First Chaplain (1946–48; 1950–53)

In fall 1946 Gould established the chaplain position, initially titled Counselor in Religion, which was described under "Religious Activities" and "Personnel Services — Counseling" in the 1946 catalog as "available to assist students with personal and religious problems and to co-ordinate all campus religious activities."[75] Carleton's first chaplain, Philip Phenix, was introduced to the college alumni in the September 1946 *Voice*:

New Religious Counselor

A NEW POST on the Carleton faculty — the position of Counselor in Religion — has been filled by the appointment of Lieutenant Philip Henry Phenix, who has recently been discharged from his duties as a chaplain in the United States Army Air Forces. Mr. Phenix, who is an ordained minister in the Presbyterian Church, holds rank in the Carleton faculty as Assistant Professor of Philosophy and Religion. In his capacity as Counselor in Religion, he has direction of the College's chapel and vesper program and serves other religious interests of Carleton students as individuals and in groups. A graduate of Princeton University with high honors in mathematics, Mr. Phenix was an actuary for a large insurance company for five years. Deciding to enter religious work, he attended Union Theological Seminary, New York, where he earned the degree of bachelor of divinity in 1942. Mr. Phenix has had an unusual war experience having been both a private soldier and a chaplain with officer's rank. During this period, he continued his religious work in preaching and pastoral work for the synod of Illinois Churches.

He had previously affiliated himself with the Society of Friends — the Quakers.[76]

Phenix was a brilliant but modest young man and did not bring to the Midwest the notoriety he had acquired in 1934 when, as a nineteen-year-old, he wrote a senior thesis at Princeton University on "The Absolute Significance of Rotation" that was praised by Albert Einstein and reported on in the

July 26, 1934, *New York Times*. Einstein, who wrote to the then-mathematics major's professor expressing his desire to speak with Phenix, commented that "The clarity with which this young man has grasped this problem is astonishing, as is his mastery of the formal apparatus." Princeton offered Phenix a position in their Department of Theoretical Physics, but he instead took a position with Metropolitan Life Insurance, and in 1939 he was elected a fellow in the American Actuarial Society, becoming the youngest fellow at the time.

Gould liked Phenix's atypical preparation for the chaplaincy — science major, business and military experience — and his brilliant mind and his academic orientation of an educational philosopher (which he would become when two years later he left Carleton to complete a PhD in the philosophy of religion at Columbia), unlike that of the traditional practitioner minister. Yet it would be Phenix's academic passion and ambivalence about the denominational Christian church that guided his shaping of the new Carleton chaplaincy, led him to serve only two short stints as Carleton chaplain (1946–48 and 1950–53), and instead embark on a career as an academic, first as a professor of philosophy and religion at Carleton and later as a professor of education at Columbia University. In both his chaplain and faculty roles, Phenix spent his academic career questioning and reimagining the traditional role of religion, morality, and character development in American higher education. It was Phenix who would seriously challenge the denominational Christianity model for the American college chaplaincy and begin the transformation of religion on campus into a broad spirituality of ethics, meaning, and service.

Students leaving the chapel, 1946

In his first annual report, Phenix described the roles and activities of his half-time position as counselor in religion.[77] (He also held a half-time position as an assistant professor of philosophy and religion.) Conducting services and public addresses was Phenix's primary and most visible activity, and the numbers were impressive: twenty-two services conducted at Carleton, including the Sunday morning service for all new students, ten vesper services, ten Tuesday morning chapel, and ten sermons preached in community churches in Minnesota (Austin, Randolph, Northfield, Alexandria, Mankato, Rochester) and Evanston, Illinois; eleven addresses on campus, and six away in Northfield, Faribault, and the Twin Cities, for a total of nearly fifty speaking engagements in his first year.

Advising the campus religious organizations, which were increasing in number and activity as the postwar campus enrollment jumped with the return of the men, required correspondingly increased chaplain time. The YWCA was the largest organization and carried out its "customary program" of worship, study, recreation, and service; the newly re-formed YMCA had a successful organizational rebirth. The Canterbury Club made its "customary very important" contribution to the religious life of Episcopalian students, the Christian Science group met each Sunday morning in Norse Theater, and a Prayer Fellowship met early Tuesday mornings. The first two non-Protestant groups formed in 1947–48: the Newman Club for Roman Catholics was established and "some attempt was also made to organize the Jewish students into a sort of fellowship."[78] Also forming that year were the so-called "Religious Liberals," a group that was Unitarian and humanist "in bias" and generally opposed, Phenix wrote, to traditional forms of religious worship and belief.

Carleton may have had students before the war with such non-traditional spiritual leanings, but it took the return of the older, worldlier, war-scarred veterans and the arrival of a veteran chaplain who encouraged divergent religious beliefs before such a group appeared at Carleton.

The student group with which Phenix was "most closely associated" was the "Sunday Night Club," an interdenominational fellowship that met after vespers Sunday evenings in the Phenix home. An average of thirty-five students a week enjoyed conversation and fellowship. Phenix attributed the informal friendly home atmosphere as "conducive to the success" of the group and reminded the president of the importance of adequate informal space to entertain student groups, believing this "practice" was one of the most fruitful parts of his work as a chaplain. Phenix and his wife were appointed Danforth Fellows and received a $50 Danforth grant to pay for refreshments at the weekly gatherings. Phenix was, unknowingly, following in the tradition of Professor Fred Hill of using his home to connect with students, but like Hill he understood well the power and influence of informal relationships and interactions with students at small residential liberal arts colleges.

Phenix worked with the religious organizations on service projects, including several weekend work camp projects in conjunction with St. Olaf students and Northfield welfare agencies. These social service projects were a Carleton tradition that Phenix believed provided a "valuable means of expressing Christian social convictions." The chaplain was also busy assisting in the organization of a long list of special projects, which included Religious Emphasis Week, World Day of Prayer, a special Christmas service and a Christmas caroling group visit to

The Sunday Night Club

the Northfield Hospital, a series of Lenten prayer services, and planning for the Minnesota Student Fellowship Conference. There was also of course often time-consuming committee work: Phenix was a member of the Student-Faculty Social Committee and chaired both the Carleton-In-China and the Faculty Committee on Religious Activities.

Another of the time-consuming and important roles for the counselor in religion was, as his title suggested, personal counseling. Oddly, the annual report contains only a brief understated paragraph headed "Personal Counseling," buried on page 8, noting that "personal counseling continued to absorb a considerable amount of time" — approxi-

mately twenty-five students per week visited his office for counseling on a great variety of problems, issues of "religious faith, social relationships, vocational uncertainties, and matters of personal adjustment." That the new chaplain was in demand for personal counseling was not surprising, as there were few such campus resources available. The Counseling Center had not yet been established, so the nearly 1,200 students had only the dean of men and the dean of women, the director of the Placement Service, and now the half-time counselor in religion for assistance with personal problems.

While Phenix was engaged in his classroom teaching and his chaplaincy work of preaching and advising students and student groups, he was struggling with a larger issue, the appropriate place of religion in mid-twentieth-century Carleton, which he addressed in a four-page section of his second annual report titled "The Religious Aim at Carleton."[79] This insightful analysis of religion at Carleton began with the pointed assertion that "It appears to me that there is a need of careful and prolonged consideration of the religious aims at Carleton" and asked "In what sense is Carleton a Christian College and what is implied in that designation?" To Phenix, the recently arrived outsider, the answer was clear: Carleton was a Christian college historically with a vague sense of Christian tradition. But in practice, Phenix argued, Carleton was no more a Christian college than many of "our definitely secular sister institutions."

If Carleton truly was a "Christian College," Phenix reasoned, it would need to change three aspects of its program and policy.

First, selection of faculty would include consideration of the applicant's "Christian convictions and commitment." Although Cowling professed this approach early in his presidency, he and Gould had given this criteria "little or no weight" in the selection of the present Carleton faculty, and, consequently, Phenix observed, many faculty did not participate in the religious program or "Church life" of the college community. Furthermore, this made it very difficult to convince students that the administration was "in earnest about the Christian life" when the faculty were "on the whole so inactive in that respect."

Second, a "church-minded college" would actively recruit students interested in an institution centered around Christian ideals and the life of the Christian community. Yet church connections, Phenix observed, had no bearing on Carleton admissions policy.

Third, a Christian college would require students to take a course in the Bible, Christian ethics, or church history, and Carleton had no academic requirements for religion.

Carleton was not, Phenix concluded, a truly Christian college (though the catalog continued to say it was) but rather a secular and cosmopolitan institution that did not want to ignore its Christian heritage; the Christian message was just "one element among many in the educational diet, accomplished through the two required religious services each week." It was well to recognize, he noted, that the religious attendance requirements were the "only sense in which Carleton can be called a distinctly Christian College." For Phenix and many others this "half-hearted espousal" of Christian faith at Carleton did not ring true.

Since Carleton was clearly not a genuine "Christian College," Phenix asked, "Would it not be better to frame the religious program in terms of the true inner nature of the institution and its implicit aims?" Carleton must shed its religious heritage from the "long-departed past" when the local Congregational Church was the college chapel and admit that Carleton had changed and now needed to meet the spiritual needs of its students in ways "more truly attuned" to the college's present character. Phenix suggested that the aim of the college in religious matters should now be to "provide a broad spiritual undergirding for the whole educational program" which would be broad enough to include "Christian and Jew, Naturalist and Super-naturalist, layman and clergyman."

This new point of view would transform the college's religious services into "convocations with a spiritual emphasis." Phenix concluded that the present form of religious service was observed "almost wholly on the basis of tradition, and not out of consideration for the most effective way" of conducting spiritual education. Christian worship must be distinguished from broad spiritual education. Phenix's analysis and philosophical approach led him to argue that the college "cannot require anyone to worship. Worship must be voluntary… all-college required worship services are out of place at Carleton as she is now constituted."

Thus Phenix recommended that the Tuesday chapel service be abandoned and replaced by an "orderly, progressive, coherent series of talks dealing with important religious issues" presented by the chaplain. This spiritual education program was not worship and could therefore be required; he saw considerable educational value in the entire student body gathering weekly for a "sustained and connected program of spiritual education." Phenix also recommended greater student involvement in discussions about religion at Carleton. Indeed, even though his appraisal of the religious situation was the result of months of discussion and reflection, he admitted to the president that "by far the greatest stimulus to my considerations has been the comment of students and observation of their reaction to the present religious program."

1948

Carleton's new "counselor in religion" had rationally and forcefully argued that because Carleton no longer functioned as a Christian college, it should drop the religion attendance requirements of Sunday vespers and Tuesday chapel. Yet more importantly, Phenix had proposed that the college should strengthen the religious/moral values education program that emphasized service and devotion to good, right, and truth, a learning for a "democracy of worth" rather than one of desire.

Although his analysis and recommendations would not be fully realized for almost twenty years, Phenix gave voice to a growing sentiment, especially among faculty and students, that the college needed to move away from its Christian heritage and transform it into a broader program of spiritual education. Phenix's analysis of the 1950 religious situation at Carleton and his recommendation to move the college from a Protestant worship to a broad spiritual educational program was insightful and prescient and provided a framework and foundation for the future of the Carleton chaplaincy, from the Protestant liberalism of David Maitland (1956–86) to the multi-faith and multi-form spirituality programs under Chaplains Davis (1986–96) and Fure-Slocum (1997–present).

In his two years as Carleton's first chaplain, Phil Phenix discovered that his mind and heart and therefore his career were in academia, especially in the philosophy of education. Thus in June 1948 he resigned and enrolled in graduate studies at Columbia and two years later completed a PhD in the philosophy of education. When his successor at Carleton, James Flint, proved to be a poor fit with Carleton, Gould happily recruited Phenix back to Northfield to again teach religion courses and serve as college chaplain. However, he returned with a new title, as he explained in a letter to Gould:

> After considerable thought, I think the title I should prefer is "Associate Professor of Religion and College Chaplain." Note

Student Religious Activities Committee members with President Gould, 195

that I put the "academic" part first. I should much prefer it so rather than the reverse order as you stated in your letter….

Personally, I like my old designation of "Counselor in Religion" very much. That represents the function I expect to fulfill. But I think there is a certain public relations advantage to the traditional title "College Chaplain," which makes it preferable on the whole. The war-time associations are largely forgotten, I think.

I am glad not to stagger under the pretentious and inappropriate "Dean of the Chapel" title [author's note: the title which his predecessor Flint held]. But I also would shudder at being called "College Preacher" or "College Pastor" for various reasons.

It is interesting how much potency there is in a name or title. It seems trivial in one sense, but the symbolic affect is tremendous.[80]

While Gould apparently wanted to signal the importance of the new chaplaincy by placing it first in the title, Phenix viewed his work at Carleton as an academic professor who also served as the chaplain, rather than as a practitioner chaplain who also taught religion. Indeed, Phenix would discover midway through the first year of his second tenure as chaplain that he preferred being a full-time professor, and he was philosophically in conflict with the chaplain position. He wrote Gould that he had "high hopes and genuine confidence" returning based on his previous experience at Carleton, the "royal welcome" he received from Gould and many other friends, and his belief that his "own intellectual and religious outlook and convictions could be reasonably compatible with those expected of the chaplain."[81] However, with his return Phenix experienced an "intense conflict between my naturalistic and humanistic convictions and what is expected by way of beliefs in the Chaplain and teacher of religion in a Christian College." To avoid, as he wrote to the president, the position of being "essentially two-faced, I must breathe the air of absolutely free intellectual inquiry" and be able to "stand up as an avowed humanist without having to constantly justify my being in the garb and position of a Christian apologist." Phenix concluded that he could not continue in the capacity of the college chaplain.

Gould held Phenix in such high regard as both a teacher and chaplain that he reduced the chaplain work, taking over with other faculty the responsibility for vespers and work with the Congregational Church. Nevertheless, Phenix left Carleton two years later for a distinguished career as a professor of education at Teachers College of Columbia University, where he authored three nationally acclaimed books, *Intelligible Religion* (1954), *Philosophy of Education* (1958), and *Religious Concerns in Contemporary Education* (1959). Phenix's chaplain's work was over, though not his work with Gould and Carleton. In 1958 Gould convinced Phenix to return again and serve for two years as dean of the college.

Gould shared Phenix's desire to examine the place of religion in the college and to make the religious program as effective as possible, and through the Board of Trustees Committee on Religious Activities he invited Professor Seymour Smith of the Yale Divinity School to conduct an "intensive personal observation survey" on a week-long campus visit in November 1951. Smith's twenty-page report[82] provided an external assessment of the state of Carleton's religious program at mid-century and listed these "Positive Observations":

1. the president and his administrative staff had a "serious concern" for religion and an "active support of, and a basic sympathy with, a religious orientation for the college";

2. half of the students participate at some time in a religious organization or activity, and one-third are regularly active, with membership estimates of YWCA (135), YMCA (65), Sunday Night Club (70), Canterbury Club (30), Unitarians (30), Newman Club (25), Friends (15), and Christian Science (15);

3. all students attend the required Sunday evening vespers and the Tuesday morning chapel;

4. and the religious facilities and finances are "very adequate" — the Skinner Chapel, a "beautiful structure sufficiently large to hold the entire student body," and the Bell Foundation and Dana Lecture Funds, which were more than adequate to support program needs.

Summarizing the positive observations, Smith concluded that on the whole, the campus appeared to be "the kind of milieu within which constructive and creative religious growth was possible among students… the moral standards appeared to be high and the mores of the campus were consistent with high ethical and religious standards. One found among students and faculty widespread opinions regarding religion and even strong negative attitudes toward religion. Yet, on the whole, the emphasis was positive and healthy."[83]

The issues Smith identified as "Problems" were similar to those Phenix was raising with Gould and

the Carleton faculty, the foremost described as the need to "ascertain the religious nature of the college."

Smith found consensus among faculty that Carleton was *not* a church-controlled, fundamentalist Protestant nor "completely secular" college; Carleton was a college with a historical and current relationship with three major church bodies and

was "maintaining a basically 'liberal Protestant' tradition in its present total educational program." Hearing "wide differences of opinion regarding the basic religious aims and character" of the college, Smith concluded, as Phenix had earlier, that the most "pressing and crucial" problem for the trustees, administration, and faculty was "clarifying the religious nature of the college" and communicating the understanding to the "total college constituency."

This need to assess and reassess the "religious nature" of the college was necessitated throughout the twentieth century as American society and liberal arts colleges became increasingly secularized. But the discussions of the place of religion in the college would be especially challenging and critical at three periods in the college's history: the post-WWII years when Carleton first selected a president who was not a member of the clergy and established the chaplaincy; the 1960s when students challenged the remaining religious attendance requirements; and the mid-1980s when the retirement of the long-serving fourth chaplain triggered an examination of the need for and role of the chaplain for the late-twentieth-century liberal arts college.

Two other suggestions in the Smith report were of significance for the future of religion and the chaplaincy at Carleton. The first was that "careful reflection of the Carleton situation leads to the suggestion that there should be a separate department of religion." Three years later, Carleton moved religion out of the Philosophy Department and created the Department of Religion with the hiring of Ian Barbour. Second was the personnel assessment that it was "impossible" for one chaplain teaching twelve hours per week to at the same time provide "adequate leadership" of the chaplain's office.

Smith found it "amazing" the Phenix could maintain high quality teaching and effective leadership of his split faculty/chaplain position, marveling that Phenix "has accomplished so much is a tribute to his competence and to unconscionably long hours of work each week." Although the combined faculty/chaplain appointment would continue until 1986, Gould immediately reduced the teaching load of the chaplain, which eventually led to the establishment of the chaplain as a full-time staff position.

Phenix was the most academic of the first four chaplains, and he shaped the role more like a college teacher than as a community pastor/minister. He was reluctant to serve as an official of the Congregational Church and made the required Sunday vespers and Tuesday morning chapel less devotional exercises and more intellectual sermons about religion and spirituality. This was a significant departure from the past, but it was consistent with Carleton's strong academic mission. By the beginning of Phenix's second stint in 1950, the catalog's "Aims" statement regarding religion in the institutional mission had changed some, now reading "Carleton College seeks to train young Men and Women with a sense of the responsibilities of freedom — young citizens with informed and critical minds who have a sense of their moral and social responsibilities. Carleton College seeks to stimulate in her students an active faith in noble ideals. Toward this end she reaffirms her ancient dedication to the development of a Christian view of life."[84] With this statement the college continued to balance the two primary institutional aims: *academic* development with liberal arts knowledge and skills, and *moral* development of character, religious perspective, and social justice, though the latter aims were now more broadly spiritual and less explicitly Christian.

In the spring of 1953 Phenix left Carleton to be a program associate and treasurer of the Hazen Foundation, which supported higher education initiatives in religion and values, college student counseling, and international cooperation and was particularly concerned with the lack of value-based and religious instruction in higher education. The following year Phenix returned to Columbia and launched a distinguished career on the Teachers College faculty that was interrupted in 1958–60 by a stint as Carleton's dean of the college.

James C. Flint, Dean of the Chapel (1948–1950)

Sandwiched between Phenix's two unsettled but successful stints as chaplain was the brief two-year tenure of Dean of the Chapel James C. Flint. Although Flint's credentials — a BA from Bowdoin, a BD from Union Theological Seminary, and work with the American Council of Voluntary Agencies for Foreign Service — were modest, Gould was elated when Flint accepted his offer for the chaplain position, which he called "one of the most important responsibilities in the life of the college," and he offered him the title of Dean of the Chapel suggesting it would "focus attention increasingly on the chapel and its symbolic role in the life of the College."[85] However, Gould discovered quickly that Flint lacked the intellect and social skills that had made his predecessor so popular and effective with faculty and students. Gould found Flint's sermons to be overly sentimental and lacking in intellectual content and was dismayed when Flint failed to call a single meeting of the Faculty Religious Activities Committee, preferring instead to work closely with a "hand-picked" student-faculty group. In his first annual report, oddly written in the third person, Flint seemed dismayed with faculty indifference toward the campus religious program:

> The fact of faculty unconcern is a matter of concern to the Dean of the Chapel. This holds true not only in the matter of attendance at the compulsory services, but also in the matter of the general religious program on campus."[86]

Though concerned that he may have made a poor choice, Gould was encouraged by positive reports of Flint's work with local churches and other groups outside the college, much of his work with

students, and his planning of special occasions. Flint was young, Gould thought, and he hoped he could grow into the chaplain position.

However, after a sermon in November 1949 that Gould found especially disturbing, the president concluded that Flint could not be an effective chaplain for Carleton. Gould twice drafted letters (on

November 22 and January 13) that he never sent, "hoping that procrastination might solve the problem." The first letter expressed Gould's immediate visceral response to the November sermon which was

> taken from the *Readers Digest* and concerned the matter of man-made or super gods centered around Prince Aly Khan and Rita Hayworth. It seemed to me at the time the most unfortunate, if not the most undignified play to the galleries I have ever heard in a Vesper sermon since I have been at Carleton College.

I was honestly so embarrassed that I should have gotten up and left the service had not that gesture been so conspicuous.... A discreet inquiry among a number of students elicited the uniform response "Awful."

It is far better to have no Vesper services at all unless they can be maintained at the level of dignity consistent with the purposes of the College. Unless religion can be made intellectually respectable, then it had best not be taught at all.

I somehow have the impression, as I look back over your sermons, that this has been

1954 Faith in World Action conference sponsored by the Religious Activities Committee

my reaction in varying degrees to all that I have heard. The one referred to above reached an all-time low.[87]

The second unsent letter, drafted on January 13, had a more measured and sad tone and began

> Because I recognize the many ways you have contributed to the college the past two years, this is one of the most difficult letters I have ever had to write. But unpleasant and upsetting as it may be to both of us, I must tell you… I see no probability of you serving Carleton in the manner which your office requires."[88]

The difficulty was primarily, Gould wrote, in Flint's preaching: "on many occasions and sometimes whole sermons that were so over popularized and so immature that even your most loyal and sincere friends have just been sick at heart."

Gould acknowledged that Flint's "type" of sermon, though "unacceptable here may well make you an outstanding success elsewhere." In February, after Flint had undoubtedly difficult conversations with both the dean of the college and the president, Gould sent a "Personal and Confidential" letter[89] stating simply "I am convinced that there is no satisfactory future for you here," an oblique but official notification that his contract would not be renewed. Gould chose not to detail the issues they had discussed, only suggesting that it was a matter of poor fit: "All of us at various times in our lives are confronted with the problem of the round peg in the square hole."

Other notes in Gould's papers suggest that Flint's dismissal went deeper than simply a poor fit. In the part of the chaplain's work that Flint most enjoyed, preaching sermons, Gould felt he was least effective. The sermons were lacking in intellectual content, too popular or too much of a play to the gallery. A year later Gould wrote in a letter to Board Chair Laird Bell that he "would not under any circumstances recommend Dean Flint for a position in a college or university" and leveled a damning indictment of Flint's work at Carleton:

> …he was the most difficult person I have had here. I have never known anyone so completely subjective. It was impossible for him to realize that there could be any other point of view than his own. He had lost the respect of almost the entire faculty by the sentimentality of his approach…. The thoughtful students came to have the same opinion of him.[90]

As an example, Gould cited the Flint sermon that ended with this observation to the students: "Now when you go back to your dormitories tonight, before you go to bed, just say 'Hi, God, what do you want me to do now?'"

Flint's tenure clarified for Gould what was needed for a successful chaplaincy at Carleton. First, he now understood that a college chaplain works in an academic environment and community which required an intellectual, not sentimental or emotional approach. Students were to examine religious and spiritual issues thoughtfully, critically, embracing multiple perspectives and viewpoints. Second, the chaplain must work collaboratively to be effective and develop close relationships with faculty and students. Third, the successful Carleton chaplain must be open-minded and flexible, welcoming of different faiths and differing points of view. Unfortunately, Flint lacked each of these characteristics and was dismissed by Gould before the end of his second year.

DAVID M. STOWE, COLLEGE CHAPLAIN (1953–1956)

After the experiences with Flint and Phenix, President Gould searched for a chaplain with strong academic, ministerial, and counseling (teaching, preaching, and listening) experience and skills. He found those in thirty-four-year-old David M. Stowe, a Berkeley, California, Congregational minister with a BA from UCLA, a BD *summa cum laude* and a PhD from the Pacific School of Religion, and three years of service as a missionary in northern China. He was introduced in the *Carleton Voice*, the college's renamed alumni magazine, as "well-known on the Pacific Coast as a counsellor of college groups and as a speaker before college audiences"[91] and the author of several articles in religious magazines. With his maturity and broad experience Stowe established immediate credibility with students and faculty in his dual roles as professor of religion and chaplain.

In his first year Stowe chaired a Danforth-funded Faculty Committee to Study the Place and Strategy of Religion in Higher Education. This committee recommended that Carleton

1. add one full-time faculty member to teach courses in religion and to supervise and guide "an integrated campus program of religious activities";

2. give separate status to a department of religion, separating it from the department of philosophy;

3. increase the course offerings in religion and establish a religion major; and

4. secure the services of a person fully trained and experienced in personal counseling from a religious standpoint, to devote most of his time to personal and group counseling.

The first recommendation was essentially fulfilled in September 1955 with the hiring of Ian Barbour, who, together with Stowe, comprised 1 FTE faculty teaching religion. The Religion Department was established with Barbour's arrival, and Stowe was named the first department chair. Course offerings were immediately increased, though the major would not be established until 1961 when Bardwell Smith joined Barbour and chaplain David Maitland.

Stowe was a gifted preacher who reinvigorated the Sunday vespers program. In his first year he delivered fifteen vespers and three chapel sermons, nine speeches in Northfield, and another ten in southeastern Minnesota churches. The following year he gave thirteen vespers sermons among nearly seventy-five sermons and addresses, including guest chapel preaching at St. Olaf, Macalester, and Grinnell and thirty-one sermons at the First Congregational Church in Zumbrota, where he served as minister for the year. He chaired or participated in numerous campus committees — the Faculty Religious Activities Committee (chair), the Public Relations Committee, the Library Committee, and the Carleton Abroad Committee (chair) — and also advised freshmen students. Each fall and spring semester Stowe organized with the CSA Religious Activities Committee the Faith in World Action Conference, a long weekend visit by a distinguished religious leader.[92] All this was in Stowe's half-time chaplain role, while he was also the first chair of the new Religion Department, taught three popular courses, and with colleague Barbour strengthened the religion curriculum.

But Stowe's sense of professional calling drew him back to the national and international mission scene, and he left Carleton in 1956 to become the educational secretary of the American Board of Commissioners for Foreign Missions and, with the formation of the United Church of Christ (from the Congregational merger), completed a distinguished career by leading the United Church Board for World Ministries. Thus Carleton's third chaplain,

like its first chaplain Phil Phenix, played an essential part in establishing and strengthening Carleton's chaplaincy and Religion Department but was called to leadership roles in the national and international field of religion and education.

Ian Barbour

David J. Maitland, College Chaplain (1956–1986)

David Maitland had everything that Larry Gould sought in his chaplain: familiarity with the small residential liberal arts college, with a BA from Amherst and two years as chaplain at Beloit College; an impressive record as a scholar and teacher, with a master's degree in history from the University of Wisconsin and a doctorate in comparative religion from Columbia University, where his dissertation was titled "The Relationship of Puritanism to Educational Reform"; and extensive experience as a college chaplain with a BD from the Union Theological Seminary and five years as Congregational chaplain at the University of Wisconsin and two years as chaplain and assistant professor of philosophy and religion at Beloit.

Altogether he was an accomplished scholar and an experienced chaplain who shared Gould's liberal Protestant philosophical approach to the college chaplaincy. As Gould was accustomed to do when he found the person he was looking for, at the conclusion of an introductory visit over tea in Maitland's New York City apartment, he made an on-the-spot decision, telling the surprised Maitland "I'd like you to be the next Chaplain at Carleton College."[93] In Maitland Gould had found someone with the impressive skills and abilities of Phenix and Stowe but someone who was committed to a career as a college chaplain. The fit was indeed good: Maitland would serve as Carleton's chaplain for the next thirty years.

Maitland served as chaplain for the final six years of Gould's seventeen-year presidency and strengthened and expanded the liberal Protestant chaplaincy. The alumni were informed of the changes in the study and practice of religion at Carleton

in the two-part April 1958 *Voice* article "Religion at Carleton."[94] Ian Barbour reviewed the evolution of religion in the Carleton liberal arts curriculum, from courses in the Department of the Bible, which existed from the founding of the college through 1934, the Department of Philosophy and Religion from 1939 through 1955, and now the separate Department of Religion. The main objectives of courses in religion were to provide "an understanding of religion as an aspect of man's historical and contemporary life" and to help students evaluate their "own philosophy of life, examining their views of man, God, and the ends of human life." Barbour suggested that examination of one's basic beliefs and convictions had assumed new urgency in the increasingly secular age of Sputnik and pointed out that the aims of the Religion Department were not the same as those of the chapel program: "Within the curriculum, reflective inquiry and systematic analysis of various theological perspectives is required not only by the liberal tradition in education, but also by the pluralistic character of our culture and the importance of the development of critical judgment." Chaplain Maitland taught a course on the relation of religion to social ethics, "Problems of Religious Belief and Practice," that included recent analyses of the values of contemporary America and "critiques of the goals and ethical dilemmas of economic and political life."

In the *Voice's* second article, Maitland described the two major foci of student religious life at Carleton and the two major responsibilities of the chaplaincy, the required services of worship and the voluntary activities of the religious organizations. The worship services were certainly familiar to alumni from the previous four decades: the Sunday evening vespers continued to follow a "simple Protestant pattern" of music from the College Choir and a sermon from the chaplain, members of the faculty, or visiting ministers; and the twenty-minute Tuesday morning chapel offered more varied patterns of worship and leadership was conducted by the chaplain, college president, faculty, or students, accompanied by the Treble Singers, a "volunteer choir of women's voices." There were also additional worship opportunities with local churches in Northfield and student-led services sponsored by the YW/YMCA, the Canterbury Club (Episcopal), the Christian Scientists, and Hillel (Jewish).

Alumni, especially those from before World War II, were likely surprised by the number and variety of student religious organizations. While the YMCA and YWCA were the primary groups before 1945, the campus now had three distinct, though interrelated, types of religious organizations: the denominational, the interdenominational, and the interfaith. There were now ten denominational groups, all established to provide opportunity for association with fellow students from one's own faith tradition: the Society of Friends (Quakers), Hillel (Jewish), Christian Science, Presbyterian Fellowship, Newman Club (Catholic), Lutheran Student Association, United Student Fellowship (Congregational-Baptist), Baptist, Wesley Fellowship (Methodist), and Canterbury Club (Episcopal). There were two interdenominational groups, the YMCA/YWCA, a "local expression of a national movement," and the Sunday Night Club, a weekly forum for the discussion of religion and related subjects. All of the religious organizations and activities operated under the broad canopy of the campus interfaith organization, the Religious Activities Council or RAC. The RAC and its member organizations had recently received meeting space in the renovated chapel basement.

In 1959 and 1960 the Faculty Religious Affairs Committee intensified its perennial discussion of religion and Carleton and responded with calls to "liberalize" the existing vesper and Chapel requirements by proposing to make the Tuesday Chapel service voluntary and providing three options (Sun-day morning college chapel, a public service off campus, or Sunday evening vespers) for fulfilling the required Sunday service. The trustees and administration accepted the proposal, and it was instituted on a trial basis in fall 1959 and permanently the following year.

Canterbury Club (Episcopalian), 1955

THE CHAPEL FACILITY IN THE GOULD PRESIDENCY

Skinner Chapel and the Emily Skinner Chapel Organ were built by skilled craftsman with quality materials. Well maintained, they served the college well through the long Cowling presidency. However, by 1949 College Choir Director and Organist Enid Woodward wrote President Gould that the thirty-three-year-old organ needed major repair work. Though it was tonally "still good" the console was simply worn out, and a new console "with self-contained combination action will give the organ flexibility and insure ease of manipulation for all." She recommended a new movable console, the revoicing of two stops on the Solo organ, and the addition of new pipes on the Great and Swell, the total cost running nearly $10,000.

Woodward reminded the president of the importance of the chapel organ in the life of the college — it was regularly used in public worship at the vesper and Tuesday chapel services and for many academic occasions and was constantly in use for instruction and practice in the Music Department, which in 1949–50 boasted thirty-two students, the largest class in organ in the history of the college. The organ was consequently used more than eight hours a day, making it "in normal church organ use something over two hundred years old!" Gould readily agreed that the Skinner Organ, at the time of its installation (1916) was "one of the finest in the Upper Midwest," and the repair and replacement work was completed by 1952.

The other chapel facility improvement made during the Gould presidency was the remodeling of the chapel basement to provide "comprehensive" facilities for a campus religious activities center and the new Religious Activities Council.

When Gould retired in June of 1962, the sixteen-year-old chaplaincy was solidly established. The first four chaplains, Phenix, Flint, Stowe, and Maitland, each struggled to find an appropriate place for religion in the life of the small residential liberal arts college, how religion fit into the evolving institutional mission. The need for the chaplain position seemed undeniable, as the demand for preaching, counseling, and advising made the half-time position nearly unmanageable. For the entire academic community, but especially the students, religion was part of the Carleton educational experience. But there was growing dissatisfaction with religion being a required monolithic communal experience of liberal Protestantism. Phenix first suggested that this narrow approach to religion did not fit well with the liberal learning value of multiple perspectives and free inquiry. There was also the growing feeling that the practice of religion, the realm of the chaplaincy, should be a voluntary and personal experience. The arrival of a new president offered Maitland and the college the opportunity to continue to examine and reshape the place of religion and the chaplaincy at Carleton.

Laurence Gould at the chapel lectern, 1954

Chapter 5

From Mandatory to Voluntary Religious Life: The Maitland Chaplaincy (1956–1986)

ON SEPTEMBER 16, 1956, DAVID MAITLAND served as liturgist at his first Carleton Sunday service. President Gould delivered the sermon, "Religious Services at Carleton," and the printed program, "A Service of Worship," featured a pen and ink drawing of the chapel's south entrance on the front cover and three quotes on the back panel that reflected the importance of Skinner Chapel, religion, and the unity of faith and reason, the sacred and the secular, at Carleton:

> "Carleton College seeks to stimulate in her students an active faith in noble ideals. Toward this end she reaffirms her ancient dedication to the development of a Christian view of life." *Carleton College Bulletin*, March 1956.

> "We shall build here a cathedral, not of bricks and mortar, but of ideas, with a spire so high, lighted by a beacon so bright that it will be a guide through all the years of their lives to all who study here… " A beacon that will illuminate and tell the world that Carleton is "a twentieth century monastery of sincere, scholarly men and women of all faiths and ideas, united by the common bond of the search for truth." Laurence McKinley Gould, Inaugural Address, 1945.

> "It is difficult to recollect any pile of stone and mortar that is so alive as the Chapel. It is even more of a creator than it is of a creation. It adds to every sermon and oratorio that is given in it." Professor Ambrose White Vernon, 1919.

The subject of the sermon and the choice of program quotes were quite intentional, proclaiming to the community, and especially to new students, that the college affirmed the development of a religious

view of life, that ideas, scholarship, and learning were sacred at Carleton, and that the college community was engaged in the sacred search for truth whenever it gathered in Skinner Chapel.

Over the next five years Maitland settled into the three primary roles of the Carleton chaplain, which were described in a 1961 *Minneapolis Tribune* article "Carleton Chaplain Must Be Minister, Teacher, Adviser."[95] Maitland, whose "close cropped hair and casual campus clothes made him look more like a graduate student than a minister," explained that time was a primary challenge of the position: "There never seems to be enough hours in the morning, afternoon or night to do all that should be done." He characterized the chaplain's responsibilities as "spilling over" into four broad areas: teaching, counseling, preaching, and advising student religious groups. Maitland noted that the one remaining religious requirement was attendance at a Sunday service, the campus or a local church service or the Sunday evening vespers lecture. The aim of the required session and of the entire religion program at Carleton, he explained, was to help students "gain an understanding of the religious forces that have played a part in the society they will enter after graduation."

The time-intensive nature of the half-time chaplain's position, which challenged each of the first four chaplains, continued to increase with the steady growth of the student population and the increasing complexity of the campus religious environment. The time issue was first addressed by reducing the chaplain's teaching load to two courses and then to a single course a year and then, in the late 1960s, with the creation of an associate chaplain position.

Throughout the twentieth century the place of religion in American colleges evolved in response to the increasing secularization of American society. After World War II, especially at nondenominational liberal arts colleges like Carleton, the place of religion and the role of the college chaplain was under intense scrutiny. While the very definition of a liberal education was continually reexamined and debated, and significant change was viewed as inevitable and beneficial, the college reaffirmed its religious tradition and the conviction that religious experience was an integral part of liberal learning.

Gould and Maitland looked to other institutions for ideas and language. Princeton wrote its new students in "The Chapel and Religion at Princeton" that it was a principle of educational policy that no student "can be truly educated and at the same time religiously illiterate. Therefore, worship

Christmas concert, 1957

is essential in a comprehensive curriculum and its values are inseparable from the Princeton ideal of education."[96] Beloit College devoted an issue of its *College Trends* publication for alumni to explaining in "Religion and the Liberal Arts" that a "sense of values" was the most important characteristic of a liberally educated person and that his spiritual, aesthetic, and social values "should have developed out of an awareness of the great value traditions, and be subjected to that scrutiny which results in a coherent philosophy of life."[97] Maitland, Barbour, and the Carleton faculty were moving in a similar direction at Carleton, building on its historical religious heritage yet also expanding the meaning of religious practice to include any spiritual and value development.

From 1956 through 1963 Maitland was responsible for Carleton's weekly Sunday morning services and a Sunday evening program, about thirty a year of each. But these were now truly college, not strictly religious, events. Maitland officiated all of the Sunday morning sessions, but he had a guest preacher/speaker deliver the sermon about forty percent of the time. The Sunday evening vespers preachers were nearly all guest speakers recruited from the Carleton faculty, area ministers, and national academics and ministers. The Fall 1960 semester list of preachers is illustrative. Maitland led four Sunday morning services, religion faculty members Ian Barbour and Bardwell Smith two others, and two outside guests, faculty from the McCormick Theological Seminary and St. Anne's College Oxford, led

Passover seder, 1957

The Smith, Maitland, and Barbour Religion Department, 1962

the rest. The Sunday evening vespers featured faculty from the University of Minnesota and Creighton (Catholic) University, the president of Lutheran Gustavus Adolphus College, Carleton Board of Trustees member Reverend Howard Conn, a film ("Day of Wrath"), a student play, and a performance of the Carleton Choir.

In 1960 Bardwell L. Smith joined Ian Barbour and David Maitland as the first full-time member of the Religion Department. Smith, like Donald Cowling fifty years earlier, had four degrees — BA, BD, MA, and PhD — from Yale and experience as a church minister. Smith immediately immersed himself in campus life, including preaching each semester at Sunday vespers, and would become one of the most important and influential faculty members in the history of religion and the chaplaincy at Carleton. Smith's academic focus was ethics, though more social and institutional than philosophical ethics, which meant he was acutely interested in the ethical and social justice issues that engaged and galvanized the chaplain and Carleton students throughout the 1960s. Smith would also chair the two most important college committees regarding religion at Carleton: the 1964 Faculty Committee on Religious Affairs that recommended abolishing the last of the religious attendance requirements and the 1986 Future of the Chaplaincy Committee.

By 1961 the religion major was established, an action that Chair of the Religion Department Ian Barbour wrote "paralleled the renewed interest across the country in the study of religion, not as a denominational or evangelical enterprise, but as an important area of scholarship with its own academic integrity."[98] Like most independent liberal arts colleges, Carleton had now completed a significant transformation for the institutional role of religion. Religion as the study and practice of Protestant Christianity and the development of a Christian view of life had been replaced by religion as an academic department and field of study, and its practice, except for the single Sunday worship requirement, had been relegated to a private, voluntary matter. Student calls for ending the final religion attendance requirement increased in frequency and intensity. Yet President Gould believed that the liberalization of the religion requirement to the single Sunday choice was sufficient and steadfastly maintained the religion requirement through the end of his presidency in 1962. As the first non-cleric president of Carleton Gould did not want to abandon or weaken the college's religious tradition, and he proudly left a legacy of a continued (though liberalized) religious attendance requirement and a strong active chaplaincy.

The Chapel

The Religious Attendance Requirement: Discussion of "the Decision" (1963–64)

In 1962 John Nason, Carleton Class of 1926, Rhodes Scholar, and former professor of philosophy and president at Swarthmore College, succeeded Gould as Carleton's fifth president. In his first year he asked faculty, student, and trustee committees to review the religion program and requirement. Nason, who had joined the Society of Friends (Quakers) at Swarthmore and believed spiritual development was a vital component of a liberal education, facilitated the process and urged all to view the requirement issue as part of a much larger and complex issue which "goes to the heart of the nature of the college, what it stands for, and what it wants to accomplish," rather than as a "simple, arbitrary administrative fiat."[99] He believed that Carleton's founders had established a Christian college with the explicit intent to provide an education which would develop students' religious and moral convictions as well as their intellectual and artistic abilities.

The faculty, student, and trustee Committees on Religious Affairs (CRA) each studied, evaluated, and discussed the place of religion at Carleton and the religious attendance requirement and produced reports with recommendations. The faculty CRA, chaired by Bardwell Smith, incorporated the student committee's findings and recommendations into its report and in May 1964 submitted a "Unanimous Proposal and Recommendations" to the Board of Trustees. The two-part proposal was succinct, decisive, and expansive in its implications: "That the religion requirement be discontinued at the end of the current academic year, 1963–64; yet, the College continue to affirm its religious heritage and tra-

John Nason

dition by increasing the quality and expanding the variety of its voluntary religious program."[100]

The decision to end the religion attendance requirement was the easy part, as there was nearly universal agreement that religious worship must be a free voluntary action and a personal choice. The affirmation of the college's religious heritage and tradition through the strengthening and expansion of the voluntary religious program would be most challenging. How that would be accomplished was addressed in the report's nine recommendations.

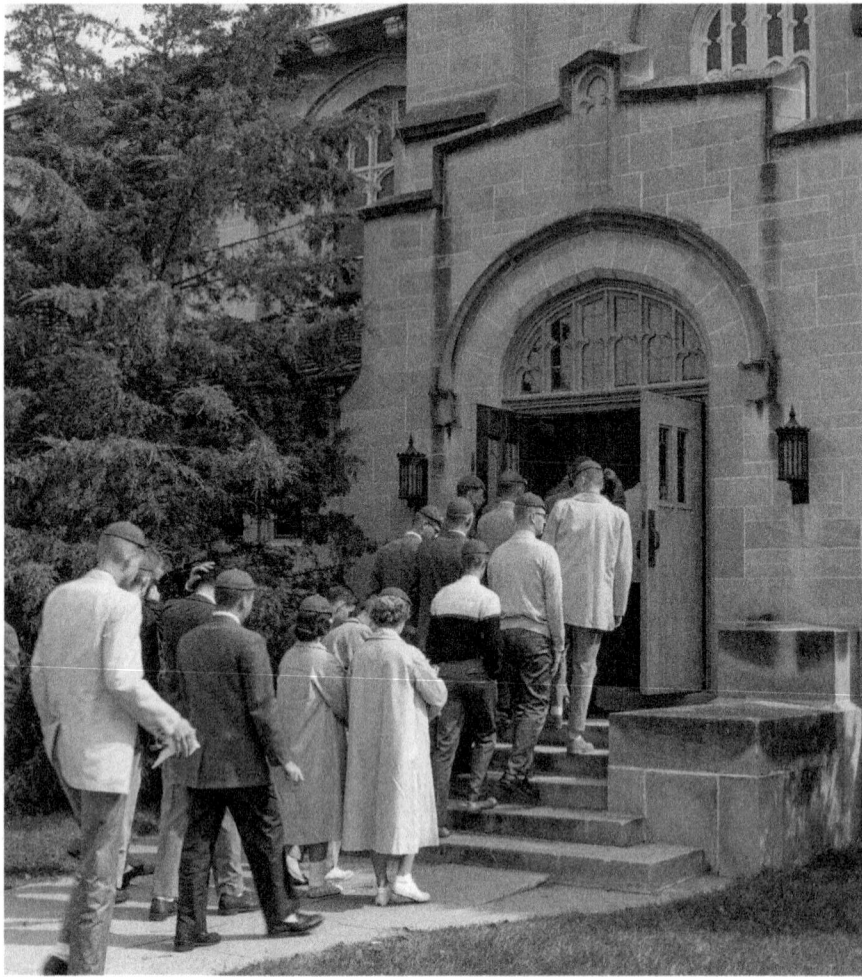
Beanie-clad students enter the chapel during freshman week 1964

Recommendation #1: "That the College continue to maintain the Chaplaincy and to hold Sunday services, together with whatever services and programs seem desirable." Although the chaplain position was nearly twenty years old, with this recommendation the faculty confirmed that the chaplain, and not the president or faculty, was the permanent college position responsible for the college religious program and student religious life. There was a place for religion and a chaplain in the college's future. This was significant, as there were some on the faculty who wondered whether the Carleton of the future, increasingly secular, pluralistic, and academically focused, any longer had need of a chaplain. "Continue to maintain" also seemed a rather mild endorsement, with no suggestion to strengthen or expand the half-time position. Nonetheless, it was a recommendation to retain a chaplain to lead and expand the college religious program.

The second and third recommendations, to establish a student Board of Religion and to continue the work of the Faculty and Trustee Committees on Religious Affairs, embedded the chaplaincy and religion program deeper into the college governance system. Now that the religion program was primarily in the co-curriculum, a student board to assist the chaplain was more in line with the Carleton tradition of student-run programs and made the chaplain role similar to that

The first five recommendations provided structure and future direction for religion at Carleton and offered a new definition of religion that would be compatible with the late twentieth- and early twenty-first-century college.

of student affairs staff. The call for an active Faculty Religious Affairs Committee representing the "diverse religious interests of its membership" signaled the institutional importance of the religion program and acknowledged the growing religious pluralism of the faculty, an invitation for non-Protestant involvement (in this era, Jewish and Catholic).

Recommendation #4, that the college **offer more support to denominational and other religious groups** recognized the religious pluralism of the student body and initiated the first efforts at interdenominational and interfaith dialog. Carleton was formally acknowledging that it was no longer a Congregational, a Protestant, or even a Christian college.

A fifth recommendation, that **the Convocation schedule each term include two or three programs with religious themes or raising religious issues,** would complete the transformation of the Sunday evening vespers into the Friday Convocation, an all-school gathering in the chapel for lectures and programs on important issues. Two additional recommendations called for increased funding to support religious speakers, by placing the Dana and Gingrich Lectureships under the faculty CRA, and for a visiting professorship in religion. All of these recommendations kept religion on the college agenda and budget, yet indicated that religion no longer had the central place or pervasive influence that it held in the nineteenth and early twentieth century under the first three cleric presidents.

Recommendations #6, #7, and #8 addressed funding and curricular issues.

The ninth recommendation, **redrafting the Aims of the College "in light of the changing patterns of liberal education and the College's reaffirmation of its own religious tradition,"** probably had the greatest long-term impact on the place of religion at Carleton, as it was in this institutional philosophical statement of purpose that the college's religious heritage was incorporated into the contemporary understanding of a liberal education. In their report appendix Smith and the CRA referenced religion in previous college "Aims" statements from the 1957, 1958, and 1962 college catalogs: "...Carleton College seeks to stimulate in her students an active faith in noble ideas. Toward this end she affirms her ancient dedication to the development of a Christian view of life" (1957) and "Carleton... aims at excellence of intellectual training, conducted in an atmosphere of Christian ethics and Christian liberalism which is her fortunate heritage...." (1958 and 1962).

A new "Aims" statement was so important to the committee's proposal that it provided a full statement of "The Aims of Carleton College" that read:

> The College has as its purpose the liberal education of young men and women. It seeks to achieve this goal by being a community in which excellence of intellectual training and breadth of understanding are sought. It is a community composed of persons who confront one another from different perspectives and within which questions of meaning and value are inseparable from the pursuit of understanding. It is, therefore, a community at the heart of which stands the conviction that education involves personal and social responsibility as well as academic excellence.
>
> The College affirms its own tradition and heritage as one which is Christian, but does not require that any of its students, faculty, or administration conform to this tradition. The issues raised by religious and philo-

sophical interpretations of man's relation to the universe are of fundamental and enduring importance for the liberally educated individual. The College therefore expects each student to concern himself with these issues, and it considers itself under obligation to provide a varied program of worship, inquiry, and instruction so that each student is able to face these issues as knowledgeably and intelligently as possible.

Through emphasis on moral sensitivity, intellectual excellence, and commitment to goals which extend beyond the self, the College hopes to send forth graduates distinguished by their ability to make critical and independent judgments, by their desire to enhance their civilization with works of their reason and their imagination, and by their will to challenge any threat to the freedom and dignity of man.[101]

On June 14, 1964, the Board of Trustees approved the committee's proposal, the nine recommendations, and adopted the "Aims of the College" statement. The statement was written specifically to provide an educational and philosophical rationale both for abolishing the last religious attendance requirement and reaffirming the importance of spiritual issues — "man's relation to the universe and questions of meaning and value," traditionally called religion — as part of a liberal education. Yet of greater ultimate importance to Carleton's future, the "Aims" statement would serve as a model for all of the major issues — governance, diversity and pluralism, social justice — that would transform Carleton in the remaining six years of Nason's presidency. The assertion that education involved personal and social responsibility to the college community inspired students and committed the college

to "confront one another from different perspectives" on issues of self-governance, racial diversity, women's rights, curriculum reform, and political anti-war protest. A renewed emphasis on moral sensitivity and concern for others, fundamental components of the college's religious tradition, provided additional rationale and passion to address these societal and campus issues. Yet perhaps most significantly, the "Aims" statement declared that the college take an educational approach, the pursuit of understanding, to address difficult potentially divisive issues. Nason and Smith, who would serve as dean of the college at the end of the decade, used this philosophical approach to lead a transformation of the college through the tumultuous 1960s. The new "Aims" statement served as the college's purpose or mission statement and was prominently displayed in the front of the annual college catalog until it was removed and replaced by the succeeding president, Howard Swearer, in 1971.

Nason felt that the discussions and changes regarding religion at Carleton were so important that in June he took the extraordinary measure of sending separate letters of explanation to students, parents, faculty, and alumni. Nason informed the faculty that the trustees had emphasized that "their decision called for increased effort... to provide new and greater opportunities for religious interest and expression" and that to underscore their concern for student religious life they had adopted the new "Statement of Aims." To alumni Nason wrote that cultural changes in American society and colleges had produced greater diversity in students and faculty and that the end of the requirement recognized the value of voluntary religious activity. The three-paragraph "Statement of Aims" was quoted in full. Nason concluded his letter with a positive

proclamation of the new place of religion in the future of the college:

> This College is committed to the liberal tradition of its founders — a tradition which combined freedom of belief with passionate concern for ultimate value. Although a formal requirement in religion has now been eliminated, we expect the religious life of students to increase rather than decrease over the next decade. The external forms of religious observance will undoubtedly diminish; the real spirit and essence of religion should increase. The trustees have au-

thorized increased expenditures for religious activities, for Sunday worship, for outstanding religious preachers and speakers. We intend to do all we possibly can to encourage students to understand their religious heritage and to go forth with a concern for the religious and moral issues of our society and time.[102]

In the end, the decision to discontinue the one remaining religious requirement *and* affirm and strengthen the religious heritage and program was, as President Nason claimed, not further secularization and retreat from the college's religious heritage, but rather a new commitment to redefine and strengthen the religious life of Carleton students. The alumni were informed about "The Decision" in an extensive article in the September 1964 *Carleton Voice*, "Discussion of the Decision,"[103] a brief introduction from Nason followed by essays by the chairs of the trustee and faculty CRAs, Reverend Howard Conn and Professor Bardwell Smith.

President Nason wrote that this "very important decision was made after long and often painful consideration of the issues, and designed not to ignore but to enrich and enhance the religious life of Carleton students." As difficult as the discussions and decision were, the greater challenge now was to "carry out the intent of trustees and faculty to encourage students to discover the significance of religious conviction and to strengthen the commitment of all Carleton students to a framework of ultimate value. This is an integral part of that liberal education which is both the tradition and the goal of the College." The proposal's nine recommendations and the "Aims" statement provided President Nason, Chaplain Maitland, and future Carleton presidents and chaplains with guiding principles and a blueprint for the place of spirituality in a Carleton liberal arts education.

The Reverend Howard Conn commended the three religious affairs committees for seeking better ways to "make meaningful our heritage," while also recognizing the growing religious pluralism in American society and on campus. The trustees heartily accepted the nine recommendations to expand the religious program in the curriculum and the co-curriculum, and Conn praised the college leaders responsible for the implementation:

> It should be noted that Carleton's Department is especially strong. President Nason himself testifies to the inner strength of the Christian faith. In David Maitland we have one of the country's finest chaplains. He commands both the respect and the interest of the students. Dr. Ian Barbour... is nationally recognized as a thinker trained in both religion and physics. Bardwell Smith, chairman of the faculty committee, is a scholar close to the students.[104]

Conn concluded by insisting that the most important component of the decision proposal was the adoption of the new "Statement of Aims" and the recognition that the college's religious heritage was an integral part of a liberal education that involved personal and social responsibility as well as academic excellence. Moreover, Conn argued that Carleton had always been a community of earnest and dedicated persons seeking meaning, value, and understanding and that historically this "sense of community and this direction of purpose have been nourished through worship in the beautiful Skinner Memorial Chapel."

Professor of Religion Bardwell Smith, chairman of the Faculty Committee on Religious Affairs, summarized the decision process and emphasized that

A Y-sponsored Easter sunrise service on Boliou Hill

redefining and strengthening the religious program was "in keeping with the rich tradition of Carleton" which "keeps its sights on the high purpose to which our college is committed," as "any college worth its salt is dedicated to dealing with matters of ultimate consequence." Carleton, Smith wrote, had the "opportunity of becoming a community in which variety of perspective is treasured and in which unity of spirit is sought."[105] Diversity was only fruitful when it contributed to "something beyond itself... when persons contribute to the whole from the richness

of their own experience and in which each person profits from the richness of others. Christians need to listen to humanists, to Jews, to Hindus, as much as vice versa. Theists need to encounter the agnostic query and the skeptic taunt, as well as the reverse."

With the abolition of the religious requirement it was now even more important that the college meet its responsibility to "encourage informed discussion of religious questions, questions which deal with the nature and meaning of life, of man, of history." That was the reason, Smith concluded, that the faculty committee proposed both the elimination of the requirement *and* the reaffirmation "in new and important ways of the College's concern for the religious dimension of its life and nature." Embedded in Smith's section of the *Voice* article, highlighted in a box, was the new "Statement of Aims."

President Nason also wrote eloquently about the place of religion at Carleton in his 1964 *Annual Report* in the section "Role of Religion," in which he summarized the college-wide discussions and the trustee decision in June 1964 to eliminate all attendance requirements for religious services and meetings. Nason believed it was a natural and positive change, and the purpose of the decision was to "enhance and deepen, not to destroy or weaken, the concern for religion on the Carleton campus."[106]

Yet the significance of the requirement decision process transcended the religion issue. Nason signaled that his administration would approach college issues and demands for change from students by creating venues (committees, community forums) to study and discuss the issue, by analyzing alternatives, and by making changes only when there was consensus that the changes would enhance or strengthen student learning and the student educational experience.

The religion requirement discussions had led the college to revise its Statement of Aims, and Nason inserted, as he had in his faculty and alumni communications, the entire three-paragraph statement in this section of the annual report. The new "Aims" statement served as a guide and touchstone for Nason's presidency and positioned the college well for the difficult issues that would come in the following six years. By defining itself as a community "composed of persons who confront one another from different perspectives" and by defining education as involving "personal and social responsibility as well as academic excellence" and expecting students to "challenge any threat to the freedom and dignity of man" the college was not only inviting, but expecting students to engage with the issues such as racism, sexism, war, and personal and social values that would define the profound transitions of American society in the mid- and late-1960s. Yet the college also expected students to exercise "moral sensitivity, intellectual excellence, and commitment to goals which extend beyond the self," that is, to address the issues with compassion, thoughtfulness, and for the greater good of the community. It was unclear to what extent Nason shaped or influenced the statement's exact language, but the message in the "Aims" statement certainly had congruence with his professed educational philosophy.

Druids. In 1964, observing that the chapel requirement could be met by attendance at any "regularly organized service of public worship," a group of students staged a quiet protest by organizing and attending their own services of public worship — a series of outdoor rituals performed under the auspices of their newly founded religion, the Reformed Druids of North America. Several of the original members were part of the Canterbury Club, advised by Bardwell Smith: faithful Episcopalians with strong feelings about religious freedom. To the founders' surprise, when the protest was no longer necessary some students chose to keep the tradition alive, and the RDNA evolved into a fairly large, serious religious organization with adherents around the world. Holding ceremonies in the Druid grove in the college arboretum, the Druids hosted celebrations for equinoxes, solstices, and other significant Druid holidays.

One of the most striking characteristics of Druidism was the degree to which it was free of dogma and any fixed set of beliefs or practices. In this way Druidism managed to offer students a spiritual path and a way of being in the world that avoided many of the problems of intolerance and sectarianism that the established religions encountered. There was no "sacred text" or the equivalent of a bible in Druidism and no universally agreed set of beliefs amongst Druids. Despite this, there were a number of ideas and beliefs that most Druids held in common, especially a belief in the fundamentally spiritual nature of life. Some Druids favored a particular way of understanding the source of this spiritual nature and considered themselves to be animists, pantheists, polytheists, monotheists, or duo-theists. Others avoided choosing any one conception of deity, believing that by its very nature this is unknowable by the mind. But whatever their specific beliefs, the early Carleton Druids maintained a healthy dose of quirky Carleton humor in their spiritual beliefs and practice.

Maitland and the Chaplain's Office were centrally involved in the various social and political issues that rocked America and college campuses in the mid- and late-1960s. Maitland's liberal Protestantism encouraged student discussion and action on issues like race relations and anti-war protests. Maitland explained his philosophy and approach to social activism in his October 1969 sermon, "Critical Loyalty," delivered after participating in a Moratorium to End the War in Vietnam march from Skinner Chapel to Northfield's Bridge Square. Some local residents had displayed American flags and "America — Love it or Leave It" signs in defiance of the protesters. These, Maitland believed, expressed an unfortunate, even dangerous patriotism and an uncritical loyalty to the country built upon the refusal of political leaders to admit error, a static view of life and politics that resisted change, and a sentimental view of love of and loyalty to country: "Few loyalties in this world are as dangerous as an uncritical attitude toward one's country, since patri-

An early Druid ritual

United Campus Christian Fellowship, 1968

otism is the modern alternative to a truly transcendent source of faith."[107]

What Maitland advocated was a "critical loyalty" to country, a self-commitment to the people and traditions of the United States, acknowledgment that historical institutions were imperfect and were not well served by uncritical devotion, and the understanding that individuals must exercise their commitment to their country by being a "loving critic of the imperfections of the society" to which they belong: "To withhold my criticism of my coun-

try is not loyalty; it could be my greatest disloyalty. To criticize may be the way that love and commitment are best expressed within the social structure."

Maitland's "critical loyalty" described the philosophy and approach that President Nason, Bardwell Smith, and other faculty and student leaders took toward the college itself. They believed that critical loyalty to Carleton meant the willingness to admit historical errors or mistakes, to take a dynamic view of life and institutions, and to embrace change to strengthen the college. Critical loyalty was the philosophical approach that allowed the college's traditional liberal Protestantism to evolve into interdenominational, interfaith, and ultimately a spiritual pluralism. The place of religion at Carleton, initially understood narrowly as Congregational and Christian practice, had expanded by the mid-1960s to a "passionate concern for ultimate value" and for developing the spiritual lives of all students.

Broadening and strengthening the place of religion on campus made the chaplaincy even more challenging and the staff position more demanding. In the fall of 1964 a half-time associate chaplain position was established, and in March 1965 Maitland sent Nason a document, "Range of Present Religious Activities: A Preliminary Account of the Work of the Chaplains"[108] that demonstrated the need for additional staff assistance for the chaplain. The seven items listed under "non-curricular" delineated the wide range of chaplaincy work: worship in the chapel, weekly Sunday morning and Tuesday noon, Holy Communion at least once per term; coordinating five or six visiting lecturers each term; advising ten denominational groups and the Inter-faith Council (IFC); conferences, on-campus, off-campus regional and national; service projects, weekly in Northfield, Hastings, Faribault, and Minneapolis; recruitment and education for church vocations; counseling, several hours per day for both chaplains, often for personal rather than "overtly" theological issues; and six faculty and college committee assignments.

Each chaplain taught two courses per year in the Religion Department. Maitland also listed eleven off-campus speaking engagements and preaching at Congregational churches in Austin, Owatonna, Faribault, Northfield, and Minneapolis. The challenge and time demands of the position were obvious when one added in the annual extensive list of speaking engagements, service on six off-campus and four on-campus committees, writing his first book on vocation and self-understanding, teaching two courses in the Religion Department, and holding weekly discussions with students in the Maitland home.

In 1967 the first associate chaplain, Joel Tibbetts, summarized the five areas of his work as "preaching, teaching, counseling, committee work, and discussion group leadership." Of his teaching Tibbets observed that "the religious climate at Carleton is favorable; studying Religion is 'in,' and consequently one finds a very broad sampling of the student body in the classroom."[109] Yet a majority of his daytime hours was devoted to "conversing" with students, though most were not formal counseling encounters: "Listening is at a premium in this community, and if one gets the reputation of being a willing listener, there will never be too few students to keep the Assistant Chaplain busy." This comment undoubtedly resonated for chaplains at Carleton and at most small residential liberal arts colleges of any era, where the personal advising relationships with students are particularly frequent and important. Tibbets concluded that Carleton was a good place to be, and the students were stimulating and responsive "parishioners." Unfortunately, the assistant chaplain position was eliminated by college-wide budget cuts in the early 1970s and not reestablished until the late 1990s.

Although the chaplaincy and the chapel program would continually increase in size and complexity through the end of the twentieth and into the twenty-first century, the chapel building itself remained, for the most part, as it had been in 1916. The Skinner Organ was renovated in 1952, and a number of

the west-side stained glass windows were replaced after a damaging June 1968 hail storm. In the early 1970s, Maitland sought to make the chapel's large formal auditorium setting more flexible and intimate, and the first seven front rows of pews were removed and replaced with removable chairs, allowing smaller groups (under fifty) to hold more informal gatherings. This minor alteration allowed the chapel to better serve its evolved purpose as the community gathering place and to function more like a New England meeting house than the gothic cathedral it resembled. The "liberated" chapel space supported both less formal, more intimate worship and "secular" community uses. The chapel's seating capacity remained the same, though changing seating standards (how closely you could pack patrons into the pews) had reduced the "practical" audience seating capacity to an estimated 900–950.[110]

The only other addition to the chapel facility during the Maitland years were six chapel banners designed by Elizabeth Barrett Hunter '41 and hand sewn by students and area women. The themes of the banners reflected the college's location and history, the daily rhythms of light and darkness, celebrated as trees, grain, night, day, and in religious symbols.[111] The sixth banner, "Joy," Maitland wrote, expressed a response to

> the God-given context of our life and work. With ecumenical intent, we exist amid farm and forest, sunlight and stars, the seasons. The banners add color to a somber building while suggesting often ignored contexts of our common life.

> The decision to emphasize the environment was intentional. While this is a Chapel, it is a college building of many purposes. Public worship is one of the activities which takes place here, but on any occasion the Chapel should help us to recover lost perspective. The banners remind us visually that our lives have a larger setting than we often acknowledge.

Having religious symbols on only one of the six banners was certainly appropriate for a facility that now served more frequently as a campus gathering place than as a place of worship.

Administratively, the Carleton chaplain continued to report directly to the president, though the chaplain formally was not a part of the president's staff and did not typically participate in the weekly staff meeting. Although Maitland and the other chaplains had close relationships with their presidents, they also operated with considerable autonomy, much more as an independent advisor than a presidential staff member. Even so, Maitland was surprised in the early 1970s when political science professor Michael Zuckert (Catholic) and math professor Sy Shuster (Jewish) suggested he view his position as accountable only to God and emphasized that "Such authority as you have

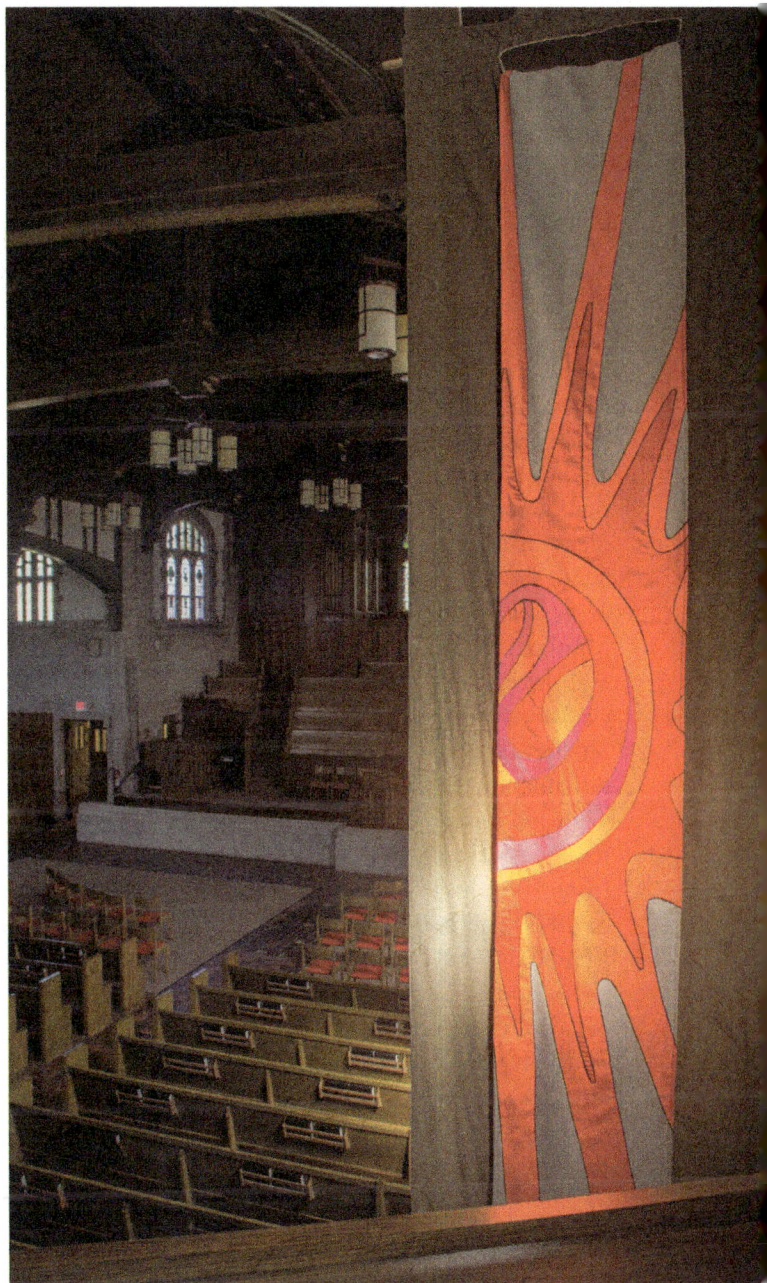

does not come from the college administration."[112] The chaplain's close but independent relationship with the president created an informal role, as one concerned with staff well-being and as a confidant, advocate, and ombudsman for faculty and staff. Maitland served in this role when he was publically outspoken about what he viewed as an unhealthy workaholism in the Carleton staff culture.

Yet it was the personal and professional rather than the administrative relationship with the president that was critical for the chaplain. Gould, although a devout, "very intense" Episcopalian who when not traveling never missed the Sunday morning holy communion service at All Saints Church or the Sunday evening vespers in Skinner, viewed the ideal Carleton chaplain to be an ordained academic, a scholar first and a practitioner second. Three of Gould's four chaplains — Phenix, Stowe, and Maitland — were exactly that and were effective and successful chaplains during the Gould presidency. James Flint, without an advanced degree or an intellectual approach to the position, had a brief, difficult, and failed chaplaincy.

In his thirty years as chaplain Maitland served four presidents: Gould from 1956 to 1962, Nason from 1962 to 1970, Howard Swearer from 1970 to 1977, and Robert Edwards from 1977 to 1986. Maitland believed he had a positive, supportive, professional relationship with all four, and was personally comfortable with and encouraged by the four men and their spouses.[113] In an interview after his retirement, Maitland recalled that Gould was a very charismatic, astute, and effective leader, though also extremely conservative and resistant to changes in American society and higher education in the 1960s: "his commitment was to hold the place together as he had inherited it" and on many issues he was "unnecessarily backward looking." Gould did establish the chaplain position and the Religion Department, but both of these changes were to strengthen the traditional Carleton religious heritage. John Nason was equally supportive and a closer personal friend and shared with Maitland an educational and political philosophy that bound them together (with Bardwell Smith) as effective institutional change agents, especially regarding the evolution of the place of religion at the college.

Maitland wrote and preached extensively throughout the 1960s about the task of building community in the increasing pluralism of society and campus and worked to make students from minority groups feel welcome and a part of the liberal, predominately white Protestant campus environment. While addressing its growing religious diversity, Maitland was also a leader in the college's nascent diversity efforts. The chaplain was also one of the founders of the college's volunteer and service organization, Acting in the Community Together (ACT), a continuation of the chapel's historical concern with service (the China Mission), community, and social justice. The monthly Black Church service, founded in 1971, featured an inter-racial Soul Choir and was often led by visiting pastors from black churches. In 1975 the student group Black Christian Organization at Carleton (BCOC) and the Third World Affairs Office led an active vital Black Church program. However, by June of 1981 Maitland wrote BCOC leaders questioning the viability and future of the Black Church, noting that interest and energy had waned from the early years when the Black Church provided an "important opportunity for Third World people to rejoice in their own religious traditions."[114]

Black chapel service, 1985

In the wake of the late-1960s and early-1970s, during which a *Time* magazine cover famously queried "Is God Dead?" and anti-war protests roiled the nation, American society experienced a general return to societal conservatism and there was renewed interest in more traditional religion on the nation's college campuses. Between 1968 and 1978 the Carleton Religion Department doubled its staff and course offerings. In a 1978 *Northfield News* article, "Traditional God 'Reborn' on Campuses"[115] Maitland described a growing interest in "new approaches" to religion and religious diversity at

Carleton. The renewed interest was different at the two Northfield colleges, however. St. Olaf's pastor Clifford Swanson said his students now possessed a "particular kind of piety" and were generally conservative, evangelical, and simplistic in their religious attitudes, making the "mood" at St. Olaf resemble the 1950s. In contrast, at Carleton the rising religious interest was in new approaches, diversity, and a renewed willingness among students to confront religious issues. Religion at Carleton was fulfilling the vision of the 1964 "Aims" statement, as more students concerned themselves with religious issues and, in the words of the statement, "confronted one another from different perspectives and within which questions of meaning and value are inseparable from the pursuit of understanding."

Ironically, however, in his second year (1971) President Swearer removed the "Aims" statement from the catalog and replaced it with a three-paragraph section titled "The Community," a vague, general statement that abandoned all but the final sentence of the "Aims" statement and suggested that the "definition of a Carleton education has approximately 1,500 variations" — a statement intended to emphasize that diversity and individuality were a "natural part of the College's purpose." There were no references to religion, spirituality, or the issues "raised by religious and philosophical interpretations of man's relation to the universe." Swearer did acknowledge that community spirit was evident in the "candid and sometimes painful sharing" (replacing the 1960s' rhetoric, "confronting") between community members, but this was an introduction to a detailed section on the newly installed governance system. Maitland noticed and inquired about the dramatic change in the statement of purpose, to which Swearer responded:

To be honest, I am not completely clear why it was dropped. The reason, in large measure, as I recall, was because it was so general as to have little meaning; and it sounded like those in hundreds of other catalogs. I, personally, have no strong feelings one way or another. If you think we should put it back in, I will be happy to so instruct Jane Koelges [director of publications at the college]. Or, we could appoint a committee to write a new statement — which would result, in all likelihood, in something very similar to the one used in recent years.

Swearer's somewhat disingenuous response revealed a surprising ignorance of recent Carleton institutional history; he did not acknowledge that the "Aims" was a carefully crafted, intentionally worded, and widely supported (by students, faculty, the previous president, trustees, and alumni) college statement of purpose defining a new place for religion and spirituality in the college's mission. Such statements don't simply get dropped. It seems more likely that Swearer, a young (thirty-eight) political scientist with no experience at a small residential liberal arts college, did not understand the importance of the statement nor of spiritual/moral/ethical issues at Carleton. It is also notable that Swearer made the change immediately after Bardwell Smith, the "Aims" statement primary author, resigned as dean of the college and returned to the Religion Department.

This episode underscored the critically important role the president has played with religion and the chaplaincy at Carleton. For the first three presidents, each ordained clergy, the impact was overt and obvious: religion and the spiritual was an integral part of their understanding of a liberal education, and it was clear to them that this liberal arts college was indeed also a Christian college. For Gould, religion was an important part of his life, and it seemed only natural that the religious lives of Carleton students were important to their overall educational experience. Nason, with his Carleton undergraduate experience under Cowling, his training as a philosopher, and his Quaker conversion and presidential experience at Swarthmore, was keenly aware of and deeply committed to the spiritual dimension of a liberal education. Swearer saw the institution through academic, secular, and post-1960s eyes, and religion and spirituality was, despite the majestic Skinner Chapel, barely visible on his Carleton landscape.

Despite the resurgence of interest in religion in the 1970s, the long-term trend was a decline in the religious preference of entering students. Nationally, the religious preferences of incoming American freshman from 1966 to 2006 also declined.[116] Increasing numbers of students reported having no religious affiliation, from 13.6 percent in 1966 to 19.1 percent in 2006. A decline was reported in categories aggregated as Protestant (Christian), moving from more than half (54.5 percent) to 48.0 percent; Catholic numbers remained fairly stable; and a decline was noted for students who identified as Jewish, dropping by almost half (moving from 4.9 percent of freshmen to 2.6 percent).

At Carleton, surveys by the Office of Institutional Research and Assessment found trends that were similar, but the numbers were quite different (see chart below). In the 1970s and early 1980s, 25 to 30 percent of Carleton students reported no religious affiliation; this number rose steadily to over 50 percent by 2010. Protestant affiliation declined from over 50 percent in 1974 to under 30 per cent

Freshman Religious Affiliations, 1971–2015

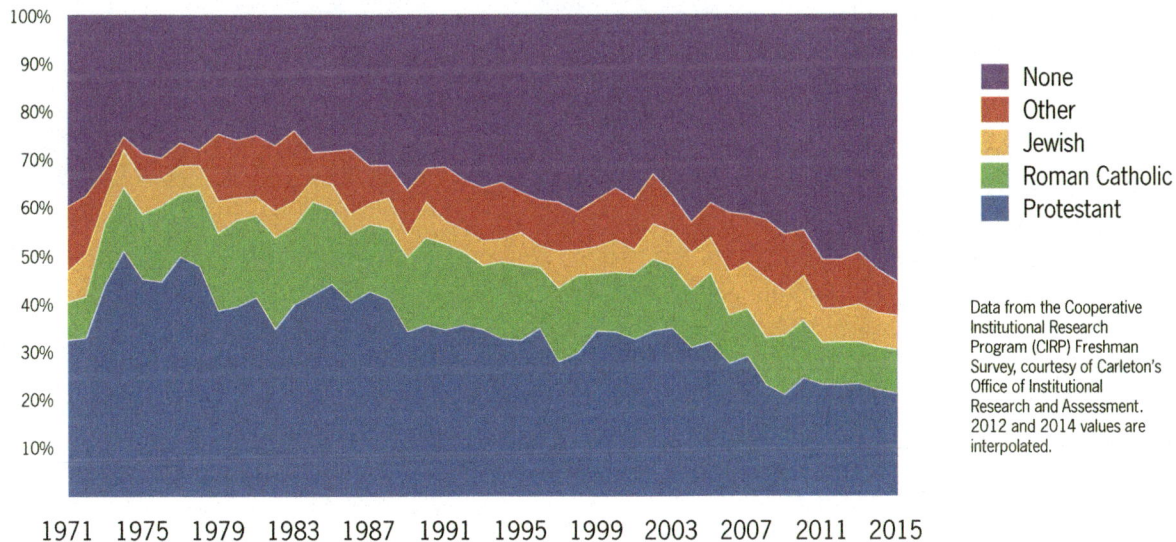

Data from the Cooperative Institutional Research Program (CIRP) Freshman Survey, courtesy of Carleton's Office of Institutional Research and Assessment. 2012 and 2014 values are interpolated.

by 2010. Catholic and Jewish affiliation remained fairly stable at between 5 and 15 percent. It was the relatively low affiliation rates, less than half of the national average, that undoubtedly convinced Nason, Smith, and Maitland to move beyond the religion of the established Christian denominations to redefining the place of religion in the context of liberal learning, to a spirituality "within which questions of meaning and value are inseparable from the pursuit of understanding."

The Freshman Surveys administered to new students since 1966 also revealed that Carleton was attracting and admitting students for whom developing a "meaningful philosophy of life" was their most important educational aim, much more than making money or success in a career. This finding suggested that Carleton students would be receptive to the college's aim of expecting students to attend to their spiritual lives.

By 1975, after twenty years as chaplain, some of Maitland's personal and professional interest and focus shifted away from Carleton and students, as he wrote two books on aging and mid-life crises, *Against the Grain: Coming Through Mid-Life Crisis* (1981) and *Looking Both Ways: A Theology for Mid-Life* (1985). Some on campus believed that the chaplaincy and the chapel program were neglected and drifting, waiting for Maitland's retirement in 1986. Yet Maitland remained an innovator and the chapel program continued to expand, fulfilling

David Maitland , 1980s

the expectations of the Aims statement twenty years earlier. The regular Sunday *Chapel at Carleton* services in 1982–83 featured term "themes" of "Wonder," "Humor and Faith," and "Turning the World Upside Down," with Maitland sharing the pulpit with faculty, students, alumni, and guest preachers. In Winter term 1984 Maitland designed and organized "Two Chapel Experiments" with the local churches. *Sunday Forums: Matters of Conscience* were a series of one-hour discussions led by Carleton faculty (Ed Buchwald, Frank Morral, Anne Patrick, Jane McDonnell, Julie Klassen, and Perry Mason). *Ecumenical Vespers* were weekly half-hour services using the Ecumenical Lectionary with music by the college choir and organists, conducted by Northfield clergy and Carleton staff and students. Both of these programs continued the town-gown legacy of the Skinner gift and the community vespers services from early in the twentieth century.

Skinner Chapel was also the venue for the weekly Carleton Convocation, which evolved from the required chapel services of the early twentieth century to the required religious-related but non-worship Sunday evening vespers of the 1940s and 1950s, to the required secular convocations of the 1960s, and finally after 1968 the voluntary Friday morning convocations that featured national and international speakers and musical performers. The Carleton Convocation series brought the college community and townspeople together weekly. The Opening Convocation and the May Honors Convocation included an academic procession and a salutatory and valedictory reading from the chaplain. Notable lecturers have included Buckminster Fuller (1968), Laurence Gould "(Science and the Human Condition," 1971), Saul Alinski (1972), Paul Wellstone ("Education and Empowerment," 1992), and Barack Obama ("Politics, Race, and the Common Good," 1999).

THE FUTURE OF THE CHAPLAINCY COMMITTEE (1985–86)

In 1985 President Robert Edwards, prompted by David Maitland's retirement announcement, asked Professor of Religion Bardwell Smith to chair a small faculty committee to review the forty-year-old position of college chaplain. In the charge letter to Smith, Edwards posed the question, "Why does a non-sectarian institution concerned with the intellectual development of students enter the domain of religion — beyond that embraced by its Department of Religion?"[117] And he promptly answered it, "Because it can provide certain resources and avenues not found elsewhere in the College: the value of reflection and calm; the idea of service to one's fellows; the beauty of liturgical music and literature; coming to terms with marriage, grief, loneliness, competitiveness, meaning, and the fact of belief and faith."

The message to the committee was clear: examine and recommend what should be the place of religion in the co-curricular lives of students rather than whether there be a place and envision and describe what should be the nature of the future chaplaincy rather than deciding should Carleton have a chaplain. Named to the committee were: Bardwell Smith, professor of religion and Asian studies (chair); Linda Clader, associate professor of classical languages; Louis Newman, assistant professor of religion and director of the Judaic Studies Program; Frank Wolf, professor of mathematics; and, representing the administration, Assistant to the President Diane Harrison and Dean of Students Cris Roosenraad.

The committee's work and report constituted the college's fourth formal review of the role of religion on campus in the forty years since Larry Gould became its first non-cleric president, preceded by the 1951 Seymour Smith study, the 1959 Barbour report, and the 1964 religion requirement discussions.

Bardwell Smith

Each review and report reflected changes in American society, higher education, and Carleton that required a reimagining and adaptations to the place of religion on campus. Most importantly, each study sought to reevaluate and redefine the role of religion and the chaplain within the purpose and mission of the college. The committee began by reviewing each of the documents from the previous studies and then met seventeen times in the winter and spring terms of 1985, meeting in twelve sessions with others, including President Edwards (twice), a trustee committee (twice), Chaplain Maitland, a consultant on community service and internships from Yale, St. Olaf Chaplain Bruce Benson, representatives from Carleton student religious organizations, college counselors, Northfield clergy, and seven Carleton faculty members representing twenty-seven faculty who signed a letter recommending that Carleton abandon the chaplain position.

The faculty group suggested that the committee was working under a mistaken assumption; it had concluded "Carleton does not need a chaplain; Carleton needs not to have a chaplain."[118] The letter argued the chaplaincy was an "alienating factor" in the college's life as it misrepresented the character of the college and "subtly but surely implies a discrepancy between many of its members' spiritual lives and what the College officially endorses." Many of the chaplain's roles — counseling, advising student groups, and coordinating community service — could, they said, be assumed by others, including student service staff and community clergy. Given Carleton's identity as a secular institution, these faculty members saw no compelling need for a college pastor.

This view had likely been held privately by a small but growing number of faculty since 1945,

but by the mid-1980s the idea of a Christian college with a chaplain seemed to many to be anachronistic and the historic institution of official college-sponsored worship to be simply "moribund." The faculty group also objected to the practice of opening college functions with religious prayers. The committee respectfully considered the arguments of the dissenting faculty and realized that they needed to make explicit in their report and recommendations the case for continuing the chaplaincy. The committee was, however, sympathetic to the group's objection to prayers at official college events and recommended that the chaplain open official college events with a reading rather than a prayer.

The committee report proposed a future chaplaincy that recognized the college's significant social, religious, and cultural changes and addressed the growing diversity and pluralism of the Carleton community. Smith, who had chaired the 1964 Religious Requirement Committee and authored that committee report, did the same with the Future of the Chaplaincy report. Just as Smith in 1964 wrote an "Aims of the College" statement to provide a philosophical rationale for redefining the place of religion at Carleton, he now wrote an extensive "Statement of Aims" section as a foundation and philosophical rationale for redefining the Carleton chaplaincy. The committee noted that the mix of beliefs and ideologies (a "dynamic pluralism") at Carleton could "enrich the educational and personal experience of the community, if it is deliberately and intelligently addressed." Even though very little engagement of intellectual or ethical diversity actually occurred on campus, the committee members suggested that

> A small liberal arts college has a unique opportunity to become a community in

which a variety of perspectives is not only valued but fostered, in which its members are helped to transcend the boundaries of their private worlds. Diversity is only fruitful when it leads to a richer community of persons who are thereby prepared to participate more realistically and more humanely in the much more diverse world beyond its walls.[119]

Religion was being redefined by a dynamic pluralism and diversity that would define the post-1960s Carleton educational experience, a transformed college bringing together pluralism and globalism with academic excellence as central college principles.

Accordingly, for this future Carleton, the concept of chaplaincy the committee proposed was

not one which would minister to parochial, sectarian, or narrowly religious ends. Rather, it would help to serve the college's more fundamental purpose which is concerned for the intellectual, moral, and spiritual growth of its students. We believe that this sort of approach is both more profoundly educational and religious, that it honors all people equally and, at the same time, their freedom of conscience. In very real ways Carleton respects the integrity of each person, valuing not only the differences between people, but also the ways in which each person seeks to reconcile the pluralities within and to be-

A student gathering in the chapel "fellowship room," 1976

come a whole human being in mind, body, and spirit... Beyond their differences, all persons are united in having to wrestle with issues of conscience, self-respect, social responsibility, and the meaning of their life. A chaplaincy which is engaged with people in these ways will enrich and deepen the value of life on this campus, for all its members.[120]

What in the past had been Protestant doctrine and practice was now defined as a pluralistic spirituality and ethics, concerned with issues of diversity, social justice, meaning, and the development of whole persons.

The chaplain of the future, the committee argued, had an important role to play in the life of the pluralistic Carleton community: "We believe finally that religious commitment can be genuinely compatible with religious pluralism and that this compatibility is essential to any sort of healthy chaplaincy at Carleton." The need to continue and even expand the chaplaincy was clear to the committee and went beyond the religious diversity within the community. The college was responsible to support the spiritual needs of all students that arise from academic work, personal and family situations, and the pressures of residential college life, and this is most effectively provided by a chaplain who can serve as a spiritual counselor. The entire community needed the assistance of a chaplain in crises such as the death of a student, faculty, or staff member: "We are a human community as well as an academic one... and must confront, individually and collectively a whole range of spiritual issues to which a resident chaplain would be especially responsive."[121] In addition, the chaplain was needed to advise the many student religious groups, as an advocate for religious tolerance and diversity, to lead an ethics program, and

to develop and expand volunteer and community service opportunities for students.

Having established the need and rationale for a new chaplaincy, the committee made specific recommendations about the future chaplain position and Chaplain's Office. The committee was divided about the position's title. Although some thought it inappropriate to continue with the traditional Christian chaplain title for the leader of an intentionally pluralistic community and suggested "dean of religious affairs," for others the term "chaplain" remained suitable. Yet for all on the committee there was an appreciation that an unusual opportunity existed, the

> possibility of creating a form of chaplaincy (whatever it might be called) which honors and encourages religious pluralism in ways that are educationally justifiable and which can assist young men and women to respect human diversity in this area and others. Finally, we unanimously concur that a chaplain or dean of religious affairs at a place like Carleton should be a spiritually seasoned person who is at the same time genuinely committed to encouraging the spiritual quests of other persons in their own ways.

This was what they would look for in prospective candidates.

The committee identified seven core functions and responsibilities[122] for the future chaplain and Chaplain's Office:

1. to provide "spiritual counsel" to students and other members of the community;

2. to facilitate and coordinate the programs and activities of the various campus religious organizations;

3. to assist the campus community in "understanding and appreciating the religious diversity around the world";

4. to sponsor and promote opportunities for conferences, retreats, and meditation;

5. to act as a liaison to local clergy;

6. to expand and diversify the lectureship and symposium program supported by the Dana-Gringrich Fund; and

7. to work closely with those on campus who are actively concerned with community service and internships.

This list would form the foundation for the position description of the chaplain for the next thirty years.

While all but the last of these functions were part of the Maitland chaplaincy, conspicuously missing from the previous chaplain's job description was public worship. The committee made no recommendation about continuing or ending the existing college-sponsored Sunday morning service but suggested instead that the next chaplain, in consultation with the Committee on Religious Affairs, "assess the situation and be allowed to make an independent judgment."

It is here that the committee's vision of the future chaplaincy was a radical departure from Carleton's religious heritage. None of Carleton's seven previous presidents or four previous chaplains could have imagined the college without public worship. But Smith and the committee envisioned the future place of religion at Carleton in educational terms, a college concerned that students learn about religion, address spiritual issues, and experience spiritual de-

velopment, but not a place that students necessarily worshiped or practiced any specific religion. Rather, the committee was persuaded that the future chaplaincy must play a central role in the pluralistic campus community and

take a proactive stance with respect to important issues as these evolve on campus or in society. While these issues will not be religious ones in any narrow sense, they will be profoundly human issues with ethical/ spiritual implications. While a dean of religious affairs is not to be seen as the conscience of the community, nor hardly as the only one interested in these issues, he or she should have as part of his or her charge the responsibility to be vitally concerned about such matters and to help promote thoughtful discussion of them within the Carleton community.[123]

Additional recommendations accelerated the evolution of the chaplain's position from a faculty position with responsibility for the chaplaincy to a full-time staff position. The recommendation that the future chaplain's position "not be a tenurable one" acknowledged and formalized the chaplain as a full-time staff member. The new chaplain would continue to report directly to the president, but less as a line supervisee and more as an autonomous independent consultant, though one with "frequent and significant consultation" with the president. Recognizing that the work of the chaplain, especially individual counseling and group advising, was now primarily concerned with student co-curricular life, the chaplain would work most closely with members of the Office of the Dean of Students. The committee also recommended reestablishing the assistant chaplain position, noting that the college was now twice the size it was forty years earlier

The 1985 *Future of the Chaplaincy* report, along with the 1951 Smith study, the 1959 Barbour report, and the 1964 Religion Requirement report constituted the institution's most extensive and careful examinations of the role of religion and the chaplaincy at Carleton. Although each report suggested the diminishing importance and centrality of religion in the life of the institution, each report also recommended changes to deepen and strengthen the student spiritual experience. Required practice and participation in Protestant services did decrease steadily from 1900 until it was ended in 1964. Yet at each point that traditional religion was diminished, the college intentionally took measures to redefine and address the spiritual needs of students and strengthen the religious program for all students. Indeed, this is a primary thesis of this history of the religion and the chaplaincy at Carleton.

The same issue of the *Voice* that summarized the *Future of the Chaplaincy* report for alumni and introduced Jewelnel Davis as the college's fifth chaplain also bid Maitland farewell. After thirty years wearing two hats for Carleton, one as college chaplain and one as a professor of religion, Maitland declared it would be something of a relief to be free to choose his own headgear. But whatever hats he chose, the *Voice* suggested, they were certain to be worn in Maitland's distinctive style, which, whether teaching or preaching, was "designed to call forth not just a nod of intellectual understanding, but a flash of enlightenment."[124] Maitland promised an active retirement filled with writing, part-time teaching, traveling, and the continuation of many lifelong activities as a gardener, runner, skier, tennis player, and movie and theater-goer.

Even after his retirement in June of 1986, David Maitland remained a connected and active chaplain

when the chaplain's position was created and that a second campus minister would allow the appointment of a male and female and someone from the Jewish or Catholic faith or from a Black or Third World background. However, the assistant chaplain position was not reestablished, and it would be nearly fifteen years before a quarter-time associate chaplain was hired to work with Jewish students.

emeritus, teaching a course in the Religion Department, hosting new student Common Reading discussions in his home, and especially reconnecting with alumni during Reunion weekends. In October 1989 Maitland provided students a Carleton religious history lesson, writing an article, "The Chapel: A Secular Place in Ecclesiastical Garb"[125] in the *Carletonian*. The Skinner Chapel's ecclesiastical appearance as a gothic English parish church, Maitland suggested, was quite misleading, as it has "always functioned more like a New England Meeting House than like the church it appears to be." Yet Carleton's distinctive Congregational religious heritage — an anti-ecclesiastical attitude, a belief in inseparable sacred and secular realms, and the autonomy of the colleges they founded — explained why Carleton's chapel would be more meeting house than house of worship. Carleton's Congregational founders believed that the college should "hold together intellect and piety, mind and heart, in the interest of fashioning whole people" and deliver an education committed to developing both personal and social wholeness:

> Given these considerations, the decision to build a chapel at Carleton on the model of an English parish church was a mistake. Skinner is much too ecclesiastical-looking for the tradition of Carleton's origins. President Cowling was apparently overly influenced by his experience of the Oxbridge gothic style.

> From the outset, however, it was its varied usages that have characterized the building from within. To know only the medieval appearance is to be misled. What appears to be nothing but a church is, in its inner workings, more like a meeting house on a New England village green.[126]

Garrison Keillor, 1986

This Congregational heritage of the sacred and the secular as inseparable parts of the whole allowed Carleton to use its chapel as a community meeting house for secular and sacred functions and to fashion the chaplain's role as minister to the minds and hearts, intellect, and piety of its students.

When David Maitland died in 2012, Chaplain Carolyn Fure-Slocum wrote of his "profound influence" on generations of Carleton students as well as on faculty, staff, and Northfield community members and of the testimony of countless alumni recalling life-changing conversations with him. The tributes from alumni poured in. Parker Palmer '61, educator, theologian, and writer, wrote:

> During my four years at Carleton, David Maitland was one of my most important mentors. He continued to be my mentor and friend until the day of his death... When I was young, David taught me how to hold faith and reason together seamlessly, a gift for which I will always be grateful. On my last visit with him, David taught me something about how to die with a twinkle in your eye, another priceless gift. Thank you, David, for gifts beyond measure — for the brilliance of mind, largeness of heart, and generosity of spirit that helped shape my life.[127]

Another alumnus, Rick Levinson, remembered a typical experience with the chaplain:

> I was a student from 1964–1968. It was a time of great change in my life. When I asked David to help me make a life decision he calmly and with a great deal of certainty told me to go with my gut. I think that was his way of telling me to have faith and particularly faith in myself. David, I shall miss you on your bike eating an apple and loving every moment of life. You were truly a blessing to me and the entire Carleton community."[128]

Chelsea Couillard '07 experienced the Maitland connection nearly twenty years after his retirement — in a Common Reading discussion, lunches with him every term for her four years, and Reunions, when Maitland would introduce her to "other alums who returned to campus to see him, and I learned just how boundless his capacity for hospitality and friendship really was. He was such a kind and generous spirit, and he will always be an important part of my Carleton memories."

These heartfelt tributes were testimony to the powerful and meaningful connections with the chaplain that were made possible by the relationships faculty and staff develop with students at small residential liberal arts colleges like Carleton. Just as these colleges create lifelong learners, they also provide its graduates lifelong friendships.

Chapter 6

A New Chaplaincy in the Old Chapel: The Davis Chaplaincy (1986–1996)

I N THE WINTER OF 1986 THE COLLEGE conducted a national search for a new chaplain to reshape the chaplaincy at the increasingly pluralistic college and to engage its students to "wrestle with issues of conscience, self-respect, social responsibility, and the meaning of their life." The selection process was in stark contrast with Gould's 1956 hire-over-lunch approach with Maitland: after 150 applications were reviewed and five finalists "met widely" with students, faculty, and staff for two-day campus interviews, Jewelnel Davis was selected and appointed as Carleton's fifth chaplain. In the announcement to the Carleton community, President Edwards wrote "Jewelnel Davis (whose first name is pronounced Jenél) impressed everyone with her intellectual strength, character, ease of manner, and her range of interests and capacities."[129] Davis, who held an AB in religious studies from Brown, an MDiv degree from Yale Divinity School, and an MSW from the University of Connecticut, was assistant university chaplain at Colgate University and an ordained Baptist minister. At Colgate she provided personal counseling and academic advising, and while at Yale was the associate pastor of the Black Church.

There was remarkable alignment between the committee's vision of the new chaplain and Jewelnel Davis' experience and background. With an interdisciplinary degree in religious studies from a residential university similar to Carleton, divinity and social work degrees, and chaplain experience with the Black Church at Yale and at Colgate, Davis was ideally prepared to play that "important role in the life of the pluralistic Carleton community." Brown, Yale, and Colgate were all, like Carleton, residential, selective liberal arts institutions and provided credibility for the appointment. Davis had experience in the role of spiritual counselor to diverse student populations. Perhaps most important, Davis' background and characteristics were such a significant departure from Carleton's first four chaplains — she was the first female, the first non-white, and the first educated after the transformative 1960s — that her very presence made the promised new chaplaincy real and visible to the Carleton community.

The Winter 1987 *Voice* article, "Carleton's New Chaplain: A Woman on the Move"[130] introduced Davis to the college's alumni and described the new chaplaincy. This Carleton chaplain preached at three or four Sunday services each term, contributed special readings at important college functions,

counseled individual students, and taught a freshman seminar titled "Contemporary Issues and Values." Yet much of her time was devoted to campus committee work, including Acting in the Community Together (ACT), Northfield's ABC program, the Council for Religious Understanding (CRU), and the Social Policy Committee (SPC).

Davis explained that she chose a career in college ministry to "escape the sexism of institutionalized religion" and to utilize her skills in counseling and her wholistic concern for men and women. Davis was intrigued with the committee's vision for the future Carleton chaplaincy and the important place at the college for the consideration of spiritual issues,

especially the committee's affirmation of the importance of engaging all students in wrestling with spiritual issues. This theme of unity from diversity would guide Davis through her ten-year chaplaincy.

After her first year, Interim President David Porter congratulated Davis on an impressive start — for having "reshaped the chapel program... [and] established firm ties with many faculty and administrative colleagues" and for playing a crucial role in the individual lives of countless students. He was equally impressed by her talents and capabilities — expertise in her field, intellectual vigor, toughness and breadth, depth of personal and emotional concern, maturity and balance, and, especially important for success with Carleton students, an "engaging sense of fun and good humor."[131] Davis' one concern was that Sunday chapel services drew so few students, an issue that challenged all of Carleton's chaplains after the abolition of the mandatory attendance requirement in 1964.

In October of 1987 Davis delivered the opening reading at the inauguration of Stephen R. Lewis, Carleton's eighth president. Lewis, an economist with development experience in Asia and Africa and formerly provost of Williams College, placed diversity and learning from difference (which he

VOICE (Visions of Inspiration and Christian Enlightenment), a student-run gospel choir, 1988

called "uncomfortable learning") at the top of his presidential agenda and quickly formed a close personal and professional relationship with his chaplain. Davis soon carried numerous additional institutional responsibilities that included weekly meetings connected with the Social Policy Committee, the Multicultural Affairs Director search, serving as the college's sexual harassment coordinator, and with the Department of Religion. Davis assisted with the selection of student staff — multicultural peer counselors, sexual harassment advisors, and resident assistants. Within the chaplain's office, Davis met weekly with student chapel associates and the Council for Religious Understanding and daily for academic advising, advising student religious organizations, and personal counseling. The often exhausted chaplain had little time and energy for conducting Sunday services and in her second year led only two or three each term.

A grateful president thanked Davis in her reappointment letter, writing that her performance was outstanding and exemplary in every category, her work with students, faculty, parents, and friends "sensitive, firm, and understanding." Her work reaching out to those of various religious persuasions, especially the Jewish community, was effective and "bears the mark of your maturity, insight, and sensitivity. The recent hotly debated question of whether Carleton should have a chaplaincy would now," Lewis concluded, "be regarded as an absurd one by most people. You've answered it in an effective way by the manner in which you've done the job."[132]

Davis' work on sexual harassment, with advisors, with individual cases, and with educational efforts was "invaluable" to the college, which was facing a lawsuit from three students. But Lewis was most appreciative of Davis' role as a general advisor, her ability to keep him aware of important realities and sensitivities, and her willingness to provide candid assessments of difficult institutional issues. Lewis recognized his chaplain was an important advisor on many matters involving students, faculty, and staff and was grateful for the soundness and well-informed nature of her advice. By the end of the president's first year, Davis was clearly his chaplain and his advisor.

In the spring of 1989 Professor of Religion Richard Crouter chaired a combined Third-Year and Chaplaincy Review Committee that provided a thoughtful, informed assessment of Davis' first three years in the "new chaplaincy." In a letter to President Lewis, Crouter and the committee's overall conclusion was unequivocal; they prefaced the report by "stating the obvious":

> It is clear in all respects that Jewelnel's work has received as strong a review as any I can remember at the college. People here are impressed by Jewelnel and wish to be sure the college knows how much they appreciate her tremendous talents. A large number believe that her appointment here is among the finest that have been made in recent years. The task of redefining the college chaplaincy, following a period of atrophy and suspicion, is demanding in every way. That she has fulfilled the high expectations of so many diverse persons, students, staff, and faculty members, while creating new and valued roles in areas that affect our common life, is an exceptional achievement.[133]

At the same time, the remainder of the letter addressed five issues critical to Davis' chaplaincy.

The first was the perennial time issue, the "accessibility of the chaplain, diversity of functions, and

overall use of time." Davis' work with the Social Policy Committee, the Office of Multicultural Affairs, and a myriad of diversity-related tasks was urgent and time intensive and pulled her away from the traditional chaplain duties of worship and spiritual advising. Both Crouter and Davis endorsed her approach to campus ministry that was "securely anchored in a set of commitments that combine the moral, political, and interpersonal with the individual counseling and the explicitly worshipping traditions of the church." Crouter observed that Davis' role in human relations, which had received formal recognition with the addition of "Advisor on Human Relations" to her chaplain title, went "to the heart of what matters most to many persons on campus," and her multiple-issue ministry with a broad scope of activities needed to be protected and supported. Crouter might have also added that Davis was functioning exactly as the Future of the Chaplaincy Committee had envisioned and recommended. Some, however, including the student Chaplain's Associates, wondered if Davis needed to do more to be seen as a "religious woman," seeing worship-related functions and human relations and diversity work as competing demands. They had good reason to be disappointed and critical of the considerable time Davis devoted to non-religious matters, recognizing that student religious life needed to continue as the heart of the Carleton chaplaincy.

The second issue was the fading interest in the Sunday chapel service, which, in the words of Choir Director William Wells had been in a "steady and irreversible"[134] decline for nearly twenty-five years, despite valiant and creative efforts by Maitland and Davis. The trouble, Wells concluded, was with the institution of Sunday chapel service and not with the chaplain. Crouter suggested that a weekly service in the large, formal Skinner Chapel might be no longer viable and that students seeking that experience might be better served attending a local church, adding that a smaller scale service on a weekday evening might be "worth attempting." Nevertheless, Davis continued the Sunday services, though not every week, and typically to congregations of less than a hundred. The services eventually became more regular when services of other faiths — Buddhist, Muslim, Jewish — were added to the Christian services. The chaplain was responsible for arranging the Sunday services but was conducting only a handful each year.

The review letter addressed three more issues for Davis and the new chaplaincy. First was an acknowledgment of the important role of the chaplaincy as "pastor to the community" on occasions of public mourning: memorial services and counseling with affected faculty, staff, and students took a "great deal more time than anyone could have imagined." Second, the committee recommended making an effort to revitalize and strengthen the work of the advisory Committee on Religious Life, with the recommendation that students be removed from the group so it could assist students confidentially. And third, to make the enlarged and diversified new chaplaincy manageable, Davis requested the restoration of the assistant chaplain position. This request went nowhere, and the chaplain worked solo until a quarter-time assistant chaplain for Jewish life was finally added in 1999. Crouter closed the review by noting his "immense satisfaction with the transformation of the Carleton chaplaincy over the last three years."

By the end of Davis' fourth year Lewis continued to express the great admiration that the whole college had for Davis. Publically and privately, he

Chaplain Davis with other members of the Religion department, 1990

applauded his chaplain for her efforts to reach out and unify the campus, her care for marginalized groups and individuals, and her skill in comforting and counseling those in need. Davis' role continued to shift more to campus human relations work, as she led the Social Policy Committee and the College Council on a revision of the sexual harassment policy and helped to write a new statement on academic freedom and discrimination. The next year she was integral to the development of an institutional AIDS policy.

Davis had already redefined the new chaplaincy much as the 1985 committee had envisioned, leading the institution as it addressed various difficult ethical and social issues on the pluralistic Carleton campus. Davis also impressed colleagues beyond the campus: in April 1990 she was elected president of the National Association of College and University Chaplains (NACUC), and in October 1990 she was elected to the Board of Trustees of the William Mitchell College of Law.

For Lewis to place his youthful, relatively inexperienced chaplain in leadership and oversight roles was quite extraordinary and indicative of the considerable confidence he had in Davis. When in 1989 he added to her work the job of "advisor on human relations," he publicly and formally, in a letter to all faculty and staff, recognized Davis' "efforts and effectiveness in helping all of us at Carleton deal with some of the more difficult issues of human relationships, including sexual harassment, gender roles, and racial and religious intolerance."[135] He also announced that Davis would chair an *ad hoc* committee to assess whether current Carleton policies "provide adequately" for persons who feel they have been subjected to harassment, intimidation, or discrimination.

To have the college chaplain participate in these institutional policy discussions was understandable: David Maitland had been similarly involved in community social issues. Yet three years later Lewis put additional, extraordinary, administrative muscle in her human relations advisor role when he gave Davis explicit "oversight responsibility" for the college's judicial and educational efforts to address sexual harassment and assault, including the power to act in an "executive capacity" with the college's deans and vice presidents and the contracted lawyer who administered the college's sexual misconduct policy. He concluded his letter to his administrative council with yet more public praise for his chaplain and advisor on human relations:

It is important that you and others know that I have a great deal of confidence in your independent judgment as do many other individuals at Carleton. And, I trust you know how valuable your work at Carleton is — not just for me but for the entire Carleton community.[136]

Throughout the decade that she served as chaplain, Davis worked with Lewis to address three major challenges of the chaplaincy: availability and making the demanding position manageable, satisfying all of the many constituencies, and structuring a successful Sunday service. The availability question was, Lewis counseled, inevitable, as many students, faculty, and staff sought some of the chaplain's limited time. The chaplain's administrative assistant position was increased to full-time, which relieved Davis of some administrative tasks and made the office seem more accessible. Lewis also urged Davis to be more visible and keep a higher profile on campus; more opportunities to be seen could make the busy chaplain seem more available. Effectively managing her time was critical, or she would burn out; Lewis challenged his chaplain not to let it happen. A second concern, that of satisfying the many constituencies, was also unavoidable, and he counseled Davis that you can't please all of the people all of the time, yet need to be aware, and do what you can.

For the third issue, finding the right structure for the Sunday service, Lewis encouraged Davis to experiment with other formats, like moving to more student-schedule-friendly Sunday evening vespers services and to increase her preaching/public speaking profile. While applauding Davis' effectiveness with bringing marginalized student groups front and center, Lewis wondered whether Davis could get other, more mainstream students, such as athletes, into her operation. Lewis also continually encouraged Davis to take on even more campus leadership positions consistent with her important public roles as a mediator and healer. At the same time, Lewis was perhaps most appreciative of Davis' role, not visible to the public but critical, as counselor and advisor to the president.

Ironically, in May 1990, in the midst of Chaplain Davis' efforts to make the campus safer for all students, someone entered her office in the chapel through a window and dropped a knife on the floor. In a letter sent to the *Carletonian* and quoted in a letter from President Lewis sent to students, faculty, and staff, Davis explained that, "As an African-American woman who has many reasons to be in the Chapel at odd hours, I find it particularly threatening to discover a knife near my desk."[137]

She was seeking information about the incident, she noted, not to pursue disciplinary action, but rather for personal safety and peace of mind. Lewis acknowledged that the incident may not have been intended as harassment, but he urged the person or persons involved to speak with Chaplain Davis on a "strictly confidential basis."

Two days later, in an anonymous letter to students, faculty, and staff, the perpetrators (presumably students) confessed and apologized for their actions, explaining that the trespassing was not directed at Davis personally, but was the only way to get into the locked chapel for a prank. The intruders, understanding now the greater harm to the community of their behavior, wrote

> We recognize that Chaplain Davis has been a personal friend to many students and more generally that she has been sympathetic to the concerns of the student body. We regret

Jewish Students at Carleton (JSC), 1990

jeopardizing the friendship and trust that she has cultivated between us, and express our sincerest apologies toward her and the student body. We hope that in spite of our rashness the warm relationship between Chaplain Davis and the students may continue to flourish."[138]

This public apology was testimony to the respect, affection, and trust that Carleton students held for their chaplain and to the power of personal relationships between students and staff possible at small residential liberal arts colleges. This was evident at the memorial service for Professor Hill, in the memorial letters about David Maitland, and with this incident.

In February 1994 a *Northfield News* article, reflecting the town's continued interest in Carleton's chapel and chaplaincy, described Chaplain Davis' busy life and packed schedule and her chaplaincy where "ministering to the spiritual and personal needs of the community comes first."[139] Davis described her role as the community pastor, sharing in the "cycles and seasons" of the lives of students, faculty, and staff, which required that she constantly adapt to the varied spiritual needs of the diverse college community. Being welcoming and flexible was critical: "I have to be open to people who don't bring traditional religious backgrounds into the conversation. I want them to be comfortable coming as sojourners, seekers or even committed Christians."

The Carleton chaplaincy had evolved significantly in the nearly forty years from David Maitland's liberal Protestant ministry to Davis' interdenominational Christian, multi-faith (Jewish, Muslim, Hindu, and more), broadly defined spirituality. Davis felt called to service in the college community and lauded Carleton's tradition of nurturing the mind,

David Kjerland repairs a chapel window, 1995

body, and spirit. Through the chaplaincy the college offered students and staff the opportunity to explore the realm of their own personal spirituality, and Davis noted that at Carleton "religious experience may occur through listening to music, contemplating the beauty of the outdoors, or feeling the rush of adrenaline after a run in the Arboretum."[140]

This call to serve the whole person, intellectual, social, physical, spiritual, in an academic residential community defined the chaplaincy at this small, residential liberal arts college in the 1990s. Thus the new college chaplaincy was a distinctly American ministry at a distinctly American educational institution. The mission of the Carleton chaplaincy, now that the teacher and preacher roles were significantly decreased, more closely resembled that of the growing student services (or Student Life, as it came to be called at Carleton) area, concerned with the co-curricular learning and personal development of students and with helping to build an open, inclusive, pluralistic college community. This may explain why in 1995 two student members of the College Council nominated Davis for the vacant position of dean of students, citing her ability to work with all constituents in a collegial liberal arts setting. Although the college chose to only consider candidates with extensive student services experience, the next dean of students, Mark Govoni, understood the critical roles that the chaplain now played at Carleton and immediately established a close working relationship with Davis, especially in the collaborative work with the Wellness Center (Govoni viewed "campus ministry and pastoral counseling as elemental parts of our health and wellness program"[141]), the Office of Multicultural Affairs, and the sexual harassment and assault program.

Yet the chaplaincy could not be reduced to a program or department in the Division of Student Life. The chaplain's mission was broadly institutional, serving the entire community of students, faculty, and staff, as was the role of advisor for human relations. If anything, this new chaplaincy, as imagined by the Future of the Chaplaincy Committee and as implemented by Davis and Lewis with the increased human relations role, had a higher campus-wide profile and influence. The chaplain, with her counseling and human relations training and relative autonomy from the administration, proved to be an effective facilitator of discussion of difficult campus issues. And Skinner Memorial Chapel again was seen as the heart and soul of the campus, paired across the Bald Spot with the college's academic mind, the Gould Library.

On March 7, 1996, President Lewis wrote the Carleton community of a "bittersweet moment" for the institution, announcing that Chaplain Jewelnel Davis had accepted the position of university chaplain at Columbia University, and Carleton thereby would be losing the presence of "an exceptional colleague, a talented counselor, a healing presence, a committed teacher, and a real leader in improving many aspects of human relationships on our campus."[142] Lewis then listed the wide range of her many contributions in her decade-long service to Carleton: an "energetic ecumenical ministry" to students, faculty, and staff of all religious faiths; leadership in the development and implementation of our policies against sexual harassment and assault; the development of a Statement on Discrimination and Academic Freedom; outreach to and education about gay and lesbian students; "moral leadership and presence at times of campus dissention, distress, and grief"; counseling of countless individuals; and significant contributions to campus discussions and programs dealing with issues of race and gender. Although previous chaplains had served the college in similar ways, Davis had realized the future of the chaplaincy, broadening its mission to all things spiritual and placing it in the center of the college's commitment to building an inclusive pluralistic campus community.

Chapter 7

The Chapel, the Chaplaincy, and Religious Life in the Twenty-First-Century Liberal Arts College: The Fure-Slocum Chaplaincy (1997–Present)

THROUGHOUT THE TWENTIETH CENTURY, Carleton College maintained its mission and strengthened its program as a private, small, residential, liberal arts college. When the college last revised its statement of purpose in 2006, the institution's essential aim remained the same as it had always been: "The mission of Carleton College is to provide an exceptional undergraduate liberal arts education... devoted to academic excellence, distinguished by the creative interplay of teaching, learning, and scholarship...."[143] Yet the college had changed significantly in many important ways. By constantly strengthening the quality of its faculty and students, Carleton's academic reputation grew, from a top regional to one of the best, most selective, small colleges in the nation. Although enrollment has been intentionally limited to retain the educational benefits of being small and personal, it nevertheless grew consistently from 100 students in 1900 to 850 by the late 1920s, 1,000 by the 1950s, 1,350 by 1970, 1,800 by 1990, and to 2,000 in the early twenty-first century. Not only was the size of the residential student community growing, but it was increasingly diverse — by geographic origin, race, socio-economic status, and religious affiliation. This growing diversity and pluralism was a defining feature of the twenty-first-century Carleton, now reflected in the final words of its mission statement, a college "dedicated to our diverse residential community and extensive international engagements."[144]

The place of religion at the college had changed dramatically over Carleton's 150-year history and was reflected in the evolving college mission statements in the college catalog. Under its first three cleric presidents, religion was central, one of the foundational pillars of the educational institution, and in the late 1800s Carleton was "intended to be emphatically a Christian College, distinctly and earnestly evangelical."[145] By 1916 the college was "especially concerned with the moral welfare of its students" and strove to "preserve a genuine Christian atmosphere and to have all of its influences count for the development of strong and well-grounded character." By 1945, with the appointment of its first non-cleric president and then its first chaplain, Carleton still aimed to "surround its students with a religious atmosphere, provide for them favorable conditions for personal religious development, and to offer opportunities... for understanding the meaning and importance of religion." The overtly Christian language was gone, but the importance of religion within a Carleton education remained.

The year 1964 was a watershed year for religion in the college mission, with the "Aims of the College" statement in the catalog declaring that "the issues raised by religious and philosophical interpretations of man's relation to the universe are of fundamental and enduring importance for the liberally educated individual. The College therefore expects each student to concern himself with these issues." The language and practice of Protestantism had evolved to a broader exploration of spiritual life and individual student development as the appropriate place of religion. However, for many students that included worship in one of the world's faiths — Christianity, Judaism, Islam, Hinduism, Buddhism, and others. Yet surprisingly, just nine years later, in 1973, President Howard Swearer replaced the "Aims" statement with "A Community of Liberal Arts," a purpose statement that removed all mention of religion, only acknowledging that one of the specific purposes of a liberal education was to "heighten ethical sensitivity and enhance the capacity to make discriminating moral and value choices." The "Purpose of the College" statement through the 1980s and 1990s continued to make no mention of religion or spirituality, with only a vague reference to "foster[ing] a critical appreciation of our intellectual, aesthetic, and moral heritage." It was within this essentially secular institutional mission that Carleton's most recent chaplains, Jewelnel Davis and Carolyn Fure-Slocum, would serve as college chaplains.

Interim Chaplain Lisa Ebert (1996–97)

When Davis departed for Columbia in the spring of 1996, President Lewis noted that the chaplain's position had evolved and expanded over a decade "in response to her demonstrated capacities and the College's changing needs" and needed some redefinition of functions before selecting the next chaplain. To get more time for the review and a national search, Lewis appointed Lisa Ebert '87 as Interim Chaplain (the role of assistant to the president for human relations being dropped) for the 1996–97 academic year. Ebert had a Masters of Divinity from Yale and had completed all but her dissertation for a PhD in theological studies from Emory.

In a letter of introduction to faculty and staff, Ebert promised that she would continue the new chaplaincy that Davis had implemented, a desire to "continue and build on the tradition of having the Chaplain's Office serve *all* of the Carleton community."[146] Ebert listed five programs and services from her chaplain's office: advocacy within the college community on matters of social justice and human rights (which included the support of groups and programs related to issues of race, gender, poverty, and gay, lesbian, and bisexual concerns); confidential counseling (noting that the Chaplain's Office was the only place on campus where confidentially extends to faculty and staff as well as students); discussion, reading, and support groups; chapel services; and the Chaplain's Office newsletter. Although Ebert would serve only one academic year, she contributed two significant changes to the chapel program, when she moved the weekly service from Sunday morning to Sunday evening and initiated a regular newsletter, the *Skinner Memo*.

CARLETON'S SIXTH CHAPLAIN: CAROLYN FURE-SLOCUM '82

Jewelnel Davis had redefined the Carleton chaplaincy as the campus office that continued to provide opportunities for traditional Christian and Jewish worship while also leading campus efforts to address newer social issues including sexual violence, HIV policy and education, and academic freedom and discrimination. The answer to the questions posed a decade earlier — should Carleton have a chaplain and what was the appropriate role and mission for the office — had been answered. Now, President Lewis and the college asked, what would be the nature and role of the Carleton chaplaincy for the twenty-first century?

That question was definitively answered by the selection of Carolyn Fure-Slocum, a religion major from Carleton's class of 1982. Fure-Slocum had the ideal background and preparation to serve as Carleton's twenty-first-century chaplain: a religion major with an emphasis in Asian studies who was, she recalled, "deeply shaped" by her Carleton undergraduate experience, which included off-campus study in India and extensive service and community activism work, with Carleton professor Paul Wellstone (later a U. S. Senator); three years as a community organizer in rural Minnesota; graduate studies, a master's of divinity and a master's in ethics from the Pacific School of Religion in Berkeley, California; ordination in the United Church of Christ; and five years service as associate pastor at the First Christian (Disciples of Christ) Church in Iowa City,

Iowa. Fure-Slocum was selected from a national pool of ninety-six candidates, and her experience with community organizing, social justice issues, and ethics was well-suited for Carleton's chaplaincy in the new century. Professor of History Eleanor Zelliot told the *Northfield News* that Fure-Slocum had the "intelligence, the commitment to diversity, and that intangible grace which we need in a chaplain."[147]

Fure-Slocum, like her predecessors Davis and Maitland, needed to be versatile and multi-talented, adept in each of the chaplain roles as counselor, preacher, administrator, and community-builder. The *Northfield News* used the "wear many hats" image again (as it had in Maitland's retirement article) to describe the complex and multiple tasks and roles required of the chaplain. Yet Fure-Slocum immediately focused on the purpose and mission, rather than the tasks and activities, of her chaplaincy and stressed that college, which had always been an especially challenging period of time spiritually for undergraduate students, was now more than ever a time for spiritual exploration. Compared to her experience at the college fifteen years earlier, she observed that students' desire for "something more" was notably stronger. The new generation of students expressed their spirituality in more varied ways, from traditional worship to meditation, discussions on sexuality and ethnicity, and community service projects. Her primary goal as chaplain, Fure-Slocum told the *Northfield News*, was "to deepen the spiritual life of students, faculty, and staff of all different faiths."[148] The Sunday services in Skinner Chapel were also more varied than they were in her student days: in her first term as chaplain there were Christian, Jewish, Hindu, and Native American services. Finally, Fure-Slocum emphasized that on a residential campus community building was an especially important part of religious life, "building that community in which people can feel comfortable."

The October 1997 Chaplain's Office newsletter, the *Skinner Memo*, Fure-Slocum's first official communication with the Carleton community, was a positive, ebullient welcome and introduction headlined "Let's Celebrate and Expand Our Diverse Faith Community!"[149] Fure-Slocum's philosophy, approach, and style was immediately evident: spirituality is integral to the Carleton experience, comes in a myriad of forms, and resides in each individual, in faith communities, and in the whole community. The message was all about the students and the Carleton community, not the chaplain. Yet the chaplain would be everywhere, working as a teacher, facilitator, mediator, organizer, and coordinator. Fure-Slocum wrote:

> Carleton's faith communities are alive and well! I have been very impressed by the number of different faith groups on campus and by their activity and dedication. Equally impressive is the amount of real inter-faith dialog as different groups meet to talk about common concerns, learn about each other's traditions, or experience the worship of other faiths. Clearly, many people are searching for spiritual meaning in their lives as well as living out their own faith through "doing justice, loving kindness, and walking humbly with God" (Micah 6:8). These invigorated faith communities — and community — are worth celebrating!

> At the same time, we need to do all we can to reach out to the many who are searching but haven't found a way to express their faith or fulfill their need for community. And

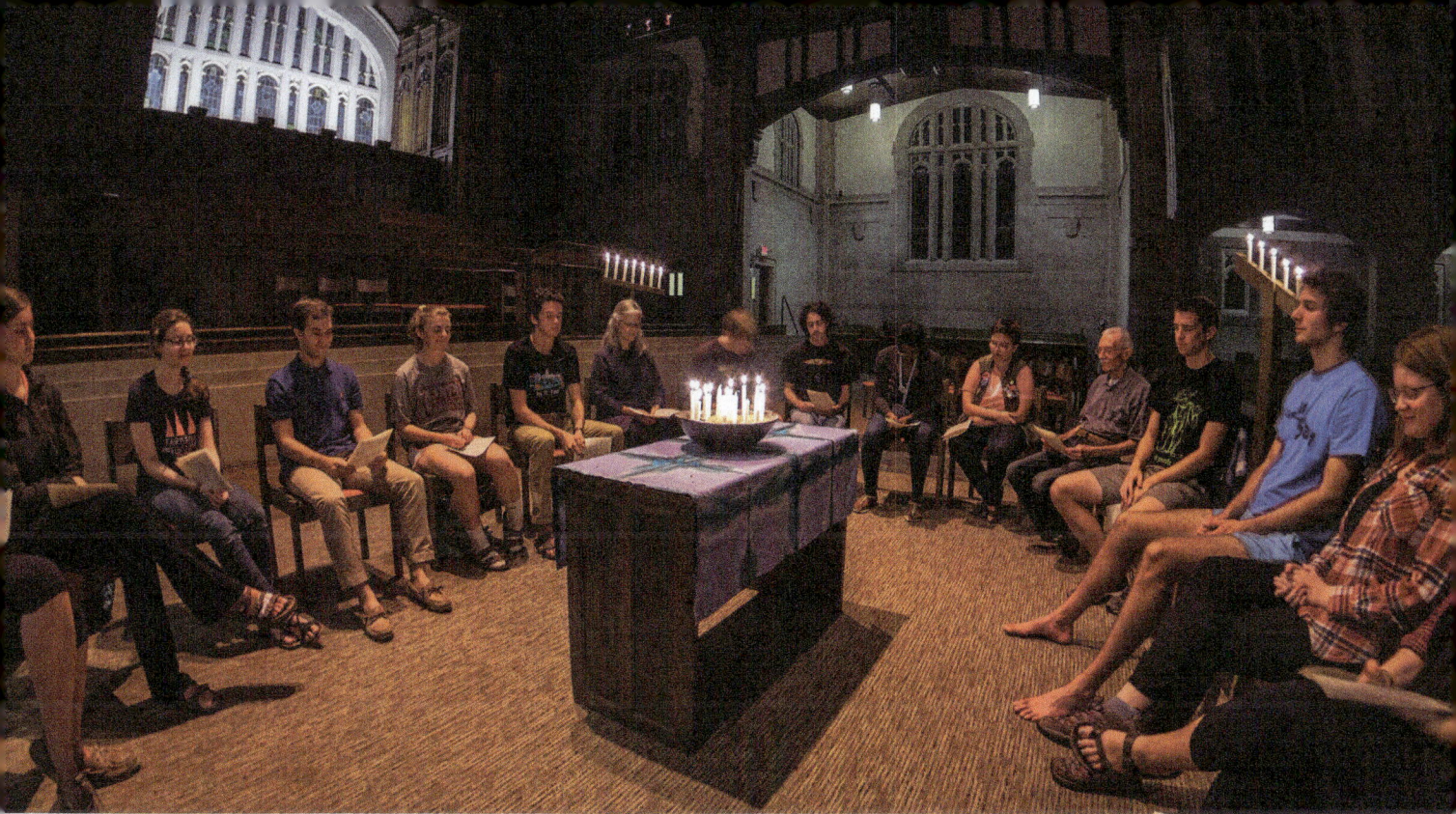

because of the terrible history of religious violence, we must continue to expand our inter-faith dialog to include more and more people. The role of the Chaplain's Office is to deepen the spiritual life of the whole campus. Hence, our celebration of what we already have here must lead us, with renewed energy, to build toward all that can be!

Thanking everyone for the "warm reception" on her return to Carleton, the letter was signed "with love and hope, Carolyn."

The resurgence of interest in spirituality and religion at Carleton mirrored the trend on campuses nationally and in American society and was similar to the religious revival twenty years earlier. Now, however, especially at Carleton, the chaplain's role was no longer about converting non-believers as it was in the early 1900s, or about supporting and encouraging Christian believers as it was in the 1970s, but rather to "encourage a spark of spirituality" across the entire institution. Fure-Slocum understood the challenges and limitations for her work; in 1998 data from the Office of Institutional Research and Assessment and other sources indicated that nearly half of Carleton's students were coming out of secular homes, 38 percent of the new students identified with no religious affiliation, and among that group some were willing to explore and some were not. Yet an unusually high percentage of Carleton students believed that developing a meaningful philosophy of life was a very important goal for their Carleton education and were therefore receptive to a chaplaincy that defined religion and spirituality as exactly that.

Although Davis and Fure-Slocum broadened the mission of their chaplaincies from supporting traditional religion to encouraging all forms of spiritual search and expression, they continued to do considerable "religious" work, in the sense of rooting the chapel services in particular religious traditions. Davis bolstered the Christian and Jewish services, while Fure-Slocum broadened the offerings to include services of many traditions. By 2000 the Chaplain's Office had expanded the number of weekly services to five: Wednesday evening ecumenical Christian Vespers (called Taizé Vespers and then EvenSong); Thursday evening Buddhist Meditation; Friday evening Quran Study and Prayers (now called Islam Inquiry); Friday Shabbat services and dinners; and the traditional Sunday evening Chapel service, representing different faith traditions each week. Only occasionally were the Sunday Chapel services "spiritual but not religious" — most came out of established religious traditions.

In her second year Fure-Slocum chose the theme of "education as transformation" and emphasized the role of spirituality in a liberal arts education, writing that "liberal arts education is about the search for meaning and understanding. Spirituality is both an end in this search and a resource for education to meet its goals."[150] To realize the college mission to "prepare people to lead a fully realized life in a diverse and changing world" required integrating all aspects of a student's life, including spirituality, in the transformative process. To begin the discussion, the Chaplain's Office launched the "Moments of Meaning Project," exploring those

Labyrinth walking meditation

"ah-ha" events when a spiritual, intellectual, political, or social idea was "understood in a larger way, or when a career or lifestyle choice became clear." The Chaplain's Office later launched the "Faculty Reflections" program series (later called "What Matters to Me and Why"), in which faculty reflected on meaning in their lives and work, to continue the dialog with faculty and students.

At the 2000 Carleton Commencement ceremony President Bill Clinton delivered the featured address, and Chaplain Fure-Slocum, as was customary, selected and delivered the opening salutatory. The national, state, and local press covered the event, writing of course about the president's remarks and the delivery by two men on horseback of the bust of Schiller, who later flew away with the president on Air Force One. That was news. But for *Star-Tribune* staff writer Eric Black, the most interesting and meaningful words spoken at the ceremony were ignored in all the newspaper coverage: it was Fure-Slocum's salutatory reading, a quote from theologian Reinhold Niebuhr that was a "challenging, eloquent, profound message to the 423 freshly minted graduates" and a "hopeful, humbling but inspiring message" for the retiring president. It is unclear how many of the graduates and audience members heard the powerful message in the salutatory, but it was testimony to efforts of the Carleton chaplain to help the college community to find meaning in the Carleton experience.

Following the legacies of Chaplains Maitland and Davis, Fure-Slocum was a leader in institutional efforts to address issues of diversity, both in her role as chaplain and as facilitator of the college's Diversity Initiative Group (DIG), later the Community, Equity, Diversity Initiative (CEDI). One DIG program included a six-week series in the winter of

2001 on "Privilege Systems: Race, Class, Gender and Sexual Orientation," an effort to "sustain and deepen conversations about some of the more difficult issues surrounding diversity."[151] The founding of DIG was yet another example of the chaplaincy and Chaplain's Office serving as an incubator for new college programs. The chaplaincy was also central in the creation of the Sexual Harassment and

Assault Committee, the LGBT Council, the Gender and Sexuality Center, and the Program in Ethical Reflection at Carleton (PERC), later Ethical Inquiry at Carleton (EthIC).

The Chaplain's Office also fulfilled a function anticipated in the Future of the Chaplaincy Report, assisting the college in times of crisis. On September 11, 2001, it responded to terrorist attacks in New York and Washington, D.C., with a special community gathering in Skinner Chapel, followed by days of silent vigil. The spiritual and emotional trauma was addressed with individual reflection, facilitat-

Chaplains Fure-Slocum, Dworsky, and Vajid at Eid al-Adha

ed discussions, and religious services, while faculty offered a series of lectures and panel discussions to examine the political, historical, and religious issues regarding international terrorism. Fure-Slocum noted that very few Carleton students retreated to their separate faith groups; rather, most in the college community sought to learn more about terrorism and about Islam. On the evening of the attacks the Carleton Jewish community invited the Muslim students for a joint service and soon after offered the use of the kitchen in the Jewish interest house for halal food preparation. Fure-Slocum thought it quite remarkable that this tragic event brought Muslims and Jews together to pray and eat, though it was yet further testimony to the inter-faith relationships possible with the intimate and inclusive environment of the small residential liberal arts college.

At the end of her fifth year, Fure-Slocum summarized in her 2002–03 Annual Report the primary roles of her 21st century chaplaincy:

> In describing the chaplaincy to those curious or skeptical folks who ask, "So what does a chaplain actually do, anyway?" I often find myself deciding between metaphors depending upon the day: wearer of many hats, gardener, utility player, shepherd, juggler, parent, dancer on thin ice, or firefighter. Further roles: priest (leading worship and other ceremonies), pastor (caring for the spiritual and emotional needs of individuals and the campus as a whole), rabbi (informal teaching and encouraging dialogue), prophet (calling individuals and the institution to consider ethical implications), and apostle (assisting religious groups in expressing their traditions, building community between individuals and between the campus and larger community). Each of these roles

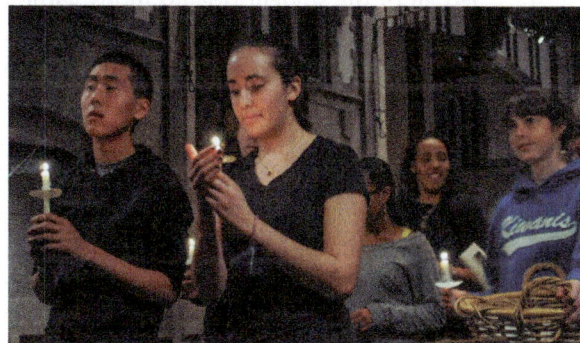

Student CAs, 2015; Diwali, 2008; Martin Luther King service, 2009

is interdependent and need to be balanced within a chaplaincy in order to deepen the spiritual and ethical life of the campus.[152]

In 2002, the Chapel staff living out these various roles consisted of a full-time, eleven-month college chaplain; a one-quarter, ten-month associate chaplain, six student chaplain's associates (CAs), and a full-time, ten-month administrative assistant. The administrative assistant position (previously called the secretary to the chaplain), had been filled by a number of people since its creation in 1962, but was anchored by Jan Truax beginning in 1989 (with a two year hiatus). The associate chaplain position was reestablished after nearly thirty years when the college's first rabbi, Shirley Idelson, was

hired in 1999. She served for two years at one-quarter time, followed by Rabbi Ze'ev Harari for one year (2001–02). After a year vacancy, Rabbi Joan Friedman served half-time as associate chaplain and director of the Program in Ethical Reflection at Carleton (PERC). In January of 2005, Rabbi Shosh Dworsky started at one-quarter-time, her position expanding to one-third-time in 2005–06 and since 2006 as half-time. In spring of 2016, the first Muslim chaplain at Carleton, Ailya Vajid, was hired at one-quarter-time. Dworsky's official title was Associate Chaplain for Jewish and Interfaith Life, and Vajid's official title was Associate Chaplain for Muslim and Interfaith Life.

The student CAs were central to the growth of the Chaplain's Office program. The position was created by David Maitland in the 1970s, in the tradition of Carleton's exemplary student employee and peer leader programs. With its student-centered philosophy, the college believed students should lead and manage most of the co-curricular services and programs. Resident assistants ran the residence halls without professional directors, and students led all of the student organizations without faculty or staff oversight. Moreover, student peer leaders were most effective at developing co-curricular programs; students learned from each other. Chaplains Maitland and Davis selected 4–5 CAs to assist them with worship services and programs, making Carleton a pioneer in the extensive use of students in a college chaplaincy.

Fure-Slocum expanded and strengthened the CA program, hiring a diverse (of religious perspective and class year) group of 8–10 students who organized the services and events, led discussion groups, and became the chaplain's arms and legs as well as ears and eyes around campus. The creativity, passion, and energy of the CAs established and sustained many of the Chapel's present programs: in 2006 four CAs established the Interfaith Social Action group (IFSA) to address immigration issues and hold discussions of social justice in each of their traditions; in 2011 CAs hosted and led regular Gospel Brunches; in 2014 CAs started, building on the legacy of Professor Ian Barbour, a Science and Religion Discussion Group; and CAs lead Religious Road Trips, discussion groups, and devotional prayer groups.

Throughout the first decade of the twenty-first century the Carleton chaplaincy continued to grow and expand, performing a variety of roles and providing a range of services and programs. Fure-Slocum's annual reports described the many components of her twenty-first-century Carleton chaplaincy.

Unitarian Universalist service, 2009; Purim, Holi, and Mardi Gras Celebration, 2

Leading or Coordinating Religious Services. Weekly chapel services from a variety of religious perspectives allowed believers of each tradition to worship in their way and for others to learn about that faith tradition. The Sunday evening service, followed by a soup supper, drew from thirty to three hundred and fifty people. Special religious holiday celebrations were arranged, and a weekly ecumenical Christian vespers service in the tradition of the French Taizé community drew fifteen to twenty people on Wednesday nights. The associate chaplain and Jewish chaplain's associate coordinated weekly Shabbat service and dinners at the Jewish Interest House that attracted ten to sixty people.

The list of chapel services for the 2008–09 academic year suggest the remarkable variety of faith traditions now worshipping in Skinner Chapel: Buddhist Meditation, Native American, Muslim Eid al Fitr, Bilingual Catholic Mass, Joint Muslim/Jewish, Mustard Seed (Evangelical Christian, each term), Diwali (Hindu), Dia de los Muertos, Sufi Muslim, Catholic Mass (each term), Martin Luther King Candlelight Service of Remembrance and Celebration, Tibetan Buddhist, Tu B'Shevat (Jewish), Quaker, Unitarian Universalist, a Multifaith Service of Music and Praise, and a joint Jewish Purim, Hindu Holi, and Muslim Mawlid-al-Nabi celebration. Notably, there was not a single Sunday service in the college's historical liberal Protestant tradition.

Fure-Slocum believed that this generation of students was more interested in organized religion than those in past decades. While she still frequently heard the "I'm spiritual but not religious" refrain, more students seemed genuinely interested in exploring religious paths. At the same time, even the more conservative of each faith tradition seemed open to learning about and from people of other faiths. While this was part of a national trend, attendance at Carleton chapel services continued to be very good compared to similar colleges, primarily, the chaplain believed, because of the chapel's pluralistic model of providing services of different

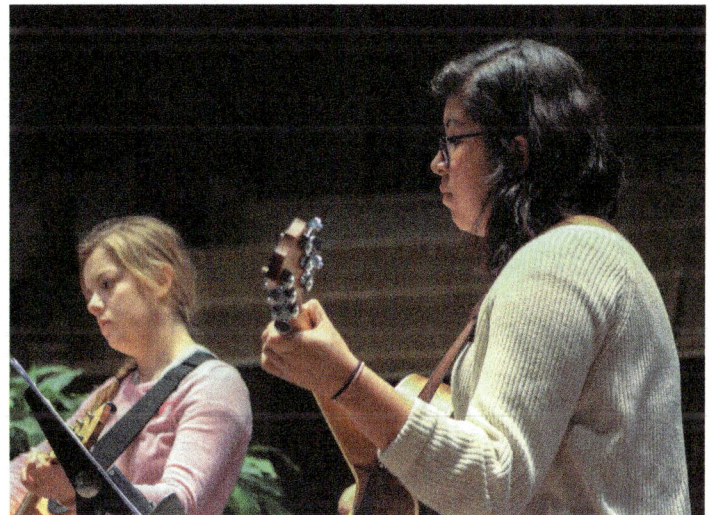

de los Muertos, 2014; Mustard Seed Praise Band, 2014

faiths each week. This model continued to meet the chapel goals of providing a real worship experience for people of that particular faith, an experiential way of learning about other faiths, and an opportunity to explore meaning broadly. The soup suppers after each service allowed for community to be built on campus. Because students often planned and led these services, they were also excellent opportunities for student leadership development.

Facilitating Discussion, Interfaith Dialogue, Meditation, and Prayer Groups. The chapel hosted a variety of single or ongoing events aimed at helping seekers to find meaning in their lives and believers to learn about other traditions or to deepen their understanding of their own faith. The Council of Religious Understanding (CRU), with representatives from the various student religious groups, met every two weeks. The chaplain's associates led one or two weekly discussion groups each term. The chapel hosted two or three "Faculty Reflections" each term, inviting particular faculty to reflect with students on meaning in their lives and work, and hosted a series called "Explorations in Meditation and Prayer."

Advising Student Religious Groups. While no student groups at Carleton have an official advisor, the chapel staff assisted student religious groups with event planning and leadership development. Many of the Christian student organizations from the Maitland years continued to flourish, including the Canterbury Episcopal Students and the Newman Club (Catholic). The humanist Unitarian Universalists and naturalist Druids continued to serve a small but active group of followers. The Jewish Students at Carleton (JSC) assisted with chapel-relat-

ed Jewish services and ceremonies, as well as hosting social and cultural gatherings to appeal to the non-religious segment of the Jewish student body. Newly established in the Fure-Slocum chaplaincy was the Carleton Islamic Association (CIA), a culturally and religiously diverse group that sponsored daily prayers, chapel services, and group meals.

Notable and surprising in the secular and liberal Carleton environment was the growth of evangelical Christian student groups. Although there had long been a small group of evangelical Christians at Carleton — the InterVarsity Christian Fellowship beginning in the 1960s, a group of students that met off-campus in the home of Dick and Carol Cover in the 1970s, the Carleton Christian Fellowship (CCF) and the Fellowship of Christian Athletes in the 1980s and 1990s — the new century saw the proliferation and expansion of evangelical groups. Coordinated by an elected panel of students, the Carleton Christian Community (CCC) helped launch new campus groups that included the Mustard Seed Praise Band,

FISH House, Praise Out, Let Love Grow, and Rest for the Weary. In 2001 Evangelical Free Church of America pastor Gary Hvass established SOul ZOne Ministries, a non-profit independent campus ministry.[153] From The Cottage on Second Street, Gary and Deb Hvass provided bible studies, spiritual counseling, seminars and retreats, prayer meetings and social gatherings. By 2009, the CCC became the Fellowship in Christ, facilitating a changing array of student groups such as Dance Like David, Wednesday Women, and Nightwatch. Many students in the evangelical student groups have historically felt marginalized, ignored, and sometimes denigrated by the college's dominant liberal Protestantism and secular humanism. However, in the inclusive and pluralistic Fure-Slocum chaplaincy evangelical students and student groups have felt more accepted and operated more visibly at Carleton.

Building Community. While all of the above activities build community on campus, the chaplain hosted additional social events, such as "Movies and Pizza" and "Turning Points," in which faculty, staff, and students gathered over dinner to talk about those "moments of meaning" that they have had at Carleton. Beyond programs, the chaplain worked to build bridges between different offices and individuals, especially within the Division of Student Affairs, and at the same time worked to link the Carleton campus to the Northfield religious community, especially by attending meetings and working with the Northfield Ministerial Association. Fure-Slocum also worked with alumni, trustees, and retired faculty and staff to strengthen their connections to Carleton and served as the primary link to the Congregational Church's successor, the United Church of Christ, in maintaining Carleton's historical affiliation.

Counseling for Faculty, Staff, and Students. The chaplains continued to serve as the only on-campus confidential resource for faculty and staff, and provided confidential counseling for students on emotional, spiritual, and career issues. This role also placed the chaplain on the Sexual Harassment and Assault team, to provide counseling when needed to complainants or respondents.

Crisis Response. Whether the issue was internal to the campus, such as hate speech or the death of a student, faculty member, or staff member, or external, such as the September 11 terrorism, the chaplain was part of the college's "crisis response team," helping to organize large or small gatherings for "making sense" of what has happened, dialogue, or grieving. The chapel also planned and led memorial services when appropriate for current or retired faculty and staff, students, and alumni.

Issue Advocacy. For both the Davis and Fure-Slocum chaplaincies when a particular issue did not have a "home" on campus, the chaplain was often called upon to initially address the concern. Davis performed this role with sexual harassment and assault and AIDS education. Because of her "umbrella" role on campus working with faculty, staff, and students, Fure-Slocum was asked by President Lewis to develop and lead the Diversity Initiative Group (DIG), a group of students, faculty, staff, alumni, and trustees involved in many diversity initiatives on campus. The chaplain coordinated the group and facilitated various campus diversity programs. The Chaplain's Office played a similar "incubator" role with gay and lesbian issues on campus, helping to create the LGBT Council (a faculty, staff, student, and alumni group), chairing the search for a half-time LGBT student advisor, and nudging forward the establishment of the Gender and Sexuality Center.

Developing Religious, Service, and Social Justice Opportunities. Together with student religious groups or the ACT, the volunteer community service program, the chaplain organized service and social justice opportunities and religious retreats. In 2008 a "Careers in Social Justice" program invited community organizers working in different types of justice concerns to talk about how they got involved, what they do, and how students could get involved now or after they graduate. Sometimes the chaplains were asked by students to get involved with social change issues. In 2007 Fure-Slocum established the Social Justice Internships, which allow 15 to 20 students to work with community organizations.

Leadership in Public Ceremonies. By the twenty-first century what was once the chaplain's most visible public role had become a small part of the job: opening and concluding readings for Open-

Jewish sukkah on the Chapel lawn; Buddhist Vesak celebration, 2013; Purim, Holi, & Mardi Gras, 2011

ing Convocation, Honors Convocation, and Commencement with a reading that can be religious but not specific to a particular tradition, that is, "spiritual but not religious." Prayers at public functions had been explicitly curtailed in 1986 as a recommendation of the Future of the Chaplaincy Committee. The chaplain was also asked to officiate at student and alumni weddings. The Carleton Chapel was typically fully booked each weekend during breaks for weddings, many of those officiated by the chaplain.

Early in her chaplaincy Fure-Slocum established the practice of holding day-long candlelight vigils, which allowed community members to acknowledge and reflect, at their convenience and in their own way, on a recent tragedy or historic event. Vigils were held annually for the September 11 attacks, Veterans Day, and Memorial Day and in response to national or global disasters and tragedies. Ten to fifteen vigils are held in the chapel most years.

A decade into her chaplaincy, Fure-Slocum's 2009 Annual Report documented a chaplaincy with a set of very similar tasks and the same mission: "supporting students of a particular religion in their efforts to live out their faith in appropriate ways; encouraging students, faculty, and staff to learn about other faiths for the sake of understanding; and helping students, faculty, and staff explore meaning in their lives, whether or not they have a religious background. Because of these broad goals, we seek a wide range of different programs to meet these needs."

After her twelfth year as Carleton chaplain, Fure-Slocum summarized her chaplaincy's mission in the report's concluding remarks, "Looking Forward":

> My thoughts about the overall goals of the Chapel remain the same from year to year: to connect the work of the mind with the heart and soul, as part of the larger Carleton educational enterprise. Because a liberal arts education is about seeking meaning in one's own life and in the world around one, spirituality and faith are an integral part of true learning. Therefore, we will continue to try to meet the needs of people of different faiths to better enable their growth, to help students to learn about other traditions and cultures for the sake of understanding, and to help all students, faculty, and staff to explore and develop meaning and purpose in their lives. To this end, we will continue to help all aspects of the Chapel program to thrive.[154]

In the fall of 2016, as the college celebrates its sesquicentennial anniversary and the Skinner Chapel's centennial birthday, the Carleton chaplaincy turns seventy years old. Fure-Slocum, reflecting on her nineteen years as chaplain, expresses immense satisfaction from seeing students grow and develop spiritually, some seeking meaning in their college experience and their lives, some questioning and exploring matters of faith, others committing to a faith community. She believes that the work of chaplain has changed considerably from her Carleton student days: much less time spent on writing and delivering sermons and more time advising student groups, assisting with student-led services, and social justice advocacy. The Chaplain's Office, like the campus community, is more diverse, open, and inclusive.

Carleton's two most recent presidents, Rob Oden and Steve Poskanzer, have continued to support an engaged and open chaplaincy. As President Poskanzer observed at the Chapel's centennial celebration dinner:

> From early on, Carleton embraced free discourse and the courageous examination of even controversial ideas. Because of this liberality of spirit, Carleton experienced a smooth transition to non-sectarianism, in due course welcoming a campus community that is drawn from a breadth of faith experiences and traditions... The Carleton community is also buttressed by a powerful chaplaincy. We have been blessed by a long line of brave and thoughtful chaplains who have embodied the highest values of the College and who have inspired us to live up to the moral imperatives of the age... Carleton students always have—and I hope they always will—wrestle with deep and enduring questions. Skinner Chapel has been a place

where we have successfully sought to help these young people answer those questions, and find purpose and fulfillment in their lives, in ways that resonate in their hearts.[155]

Despite the significant changes in Carleton and the chaplaincy, Fure-Slocum's oft-repeated mission "To help all students, faculty, and staff to explore and develop meaning and purpose in their lives" aptly describes the primary purpose of the chaplaincy of each of Carleton's six chaplains. For the first four chaplains it was Protestantism and Christian faith that supplied the meaning and purpose; for the two most recent chaplains it has been a personal and individual spirituality, which may or may not be Christian or even part of an organized religion. Yet all of Carleton's six chaplains have been dedicated to helping students explore the spiritual dimensions of their liberal arts education. While the form and format has changed, the core purpose of all six chaplaincies has been essentially the same even though the place of religion in their Carleton lives has changed significantly for students. In the late-nineteenth century, a pious Protestantism was woven into their education experience. For the first sixty years of the twentieth century a liberal Protestantism was decreasingly central to the student experience. And for the last fifty years the place of religion (or spirituality) became individual, voluntary, diverse, and multi-faith in substance and form. However, despite the fading importance of traditional Protestant religion at Carleton, the search for meaning and purpose and the development of the spiritual self has remained an integral part of the Carleton liberal arts educational experience.

Skinner Memorial Chapel, celebrating its centennial birthday in October of 2016, has changed very little. Although major infrastructure work — a new

heating/cooling system, lighting and sound systems, cleaning and repair of the exterior stone, and replacement of the red tile roof — was completed in recent years, the building is essentially the same as it was when dedicated by President Cowling in October of 1916. The walls, flooring, pews, and large oak beams are all original. Skinner continues to host regular religious services. The non-religious experience of Skinner — the official college events, the convocations, the musical performances, the community meeting hall gatherings — has been remarkably similar for generations of Carleton students.

Every Carleton alumnus has memories of Skinner Memorial Chapel. The massive gray stone English Gothic chapel, with its majestic bell tower soaring above the Bald Spot, is a campus centerpiece — whether it's covered by winter's snows or framed by summer's trees. Nearly all students have sat in the wooden pews, waiting to be welcomed to Carleton during their first week on campus. Nearly all alumni have attended a convocation, concert, or worship service in the Skinner Chapel.

The Skinner Chapel has served generations of Carleton students as Carleton's spiritual center and primary campus lecture and music performance space. It has been a space to worship and learn, celebrate and grieve, gather with the community or sit in solitary silence. The chapel experience — like the Carleton experience — is varied, individual, yet profoundly common. For thousands of Carls, Skinner Memorial Chapel is a place of memories, meaning, and music. It is those common Skinner experiences and memories that has made the Skinner Memorial Chapel a special place for generations of Carleton students and alumni.

Chapel model in LEGO created by John Hassett '00 for Carleton's Sesquicentennial

Endnotes

1 John E. Boodin, "Carleton College," *Alumni Magazine of Carleton College*, vol. VI, no. 4 (February 1916), 129–30.

2 Eric Hillemann, senior associate in archives at Carleton, wrote this description of religion and nineteenth-century Carleton for an essay titled "Earnest and Evangelical" in a photographic history for the college's sesquicentennial.

3 George P. Schmidt, *The Liberal Arts College: A Chapter in American Cultural History* (New Brunswick: Rutgers University Press, 1957).

4 Peter Gomes, "Affirmation and Adaptation: Values and the Elite Residential College," in *Distinctively American: The Residential Liberal Arts Colleges*, ed. Steven Koblik and Stephen Graubard (New Brunswick, NJ: Transaction Publishers, 2000), 101.

5 "The Yale Report of 1828" was a report from the faculty of Yale College that argued that teaching students how to think and developing in them the skills of reasoning, imagination, and critical analysis was more important than simply teaching them how to recite facts. Yale College and Robert J. O'Hara. "The Yale Report of 1828 · Part I: Liberal Education and Collegiate Life," 1828.

6 F. Thomas Trotter, "Foreword," in Merrimon Cunningham, *Uneasy Partners: The College and the Church* (Nashville: Abingdon Press, 1994), 9.

7 Kenneth Underwood, *The Church, the University, and Social Policy: The Danforth Study of Campus Ministries* (Middletown, CT: Wesleyan University Press, 1969), 56.

8 Op cit., Gomes, *Distinctively American: The Residential Liberal Arts Colleges*.

9 Bardwell Smith, "Report of the Faculty Committee on Religious Affairs," 4 February 1964, Carleton College Archives. This language was incorporated into the Statement of Aims adopted with the proposal to abolish the religious attendance requirement.

10 George P. Schmidt, *The Liberal Arts College: A Chapter in American Cultural History* (New Brunswick: Rutgers University Press, 1957); James Burtchaell, *The Dying of the Light: The Disengagement of Colleges and Universities From Their Christian Churches* (Grand Rapids, MI: William Eerdmans Publishing, 1998).

11 *Catalog* (Northfield, MN: Carleton College, 1872), Carleton College Archives.

12 *Catalog* (Northfield, MN: Carleton College, 1880), Carleton College Archives.

13 James W. Strong, "Annual Report for 1872–73, Carleton College," Carleton College Archives.

14 James W. Strong, "Annual Report for 1873–74, Carleton College," Carleton College Archives.

15 James W. Strong, "Annual Report for 1882–83, Carleton College," Carleton College Archives.

16 James W. Strong, "Annual Report for 1885–86, Carleton College," Carleton College Archives.

17 James W. Strong, "Annual Report for 1901–02, Carleton College," Carleton College Archives.

18 Leal Headley and Merrill Jarchow, *Carleton: The First Century* (Northfield, MN: Carleton College, 1966), 39.

19 *Algol* (Northfield, MN: Carleton College, 1895), Carleton College Archives.

20 *Algol* (Northfield, MN: Carleton College, 1895), Carleton College Archives.

21 Op. cit., Headley and Jarchow, *Carleton: The First Century*, 138.

22 Ibid., 236–37.

23 Throughout its history the student newspaper has been known variously as *Carleton*, *Carletonia*, the *Carletonian*, and the *'Tonian*. For purposes of clarity and standardization we will refer to it in this history as the *Carletonian*.

24 Ibid., 393.

25 James W. Strong quoted Evan's summary of the "Woman's Program" in his "Annual Report for

1901–02, Carleton College," Carleton College Archives.

26 Attributed to the Carletonian in Merrill Jarchow, *Carleton: The First Century* (Northfield, MN: Carleton College, 1966), 236–37. Ibid., 237–38.

27 Ibid., 237–38.

28 William Sallmon, "Annual Report for 1903, Carleton College," Sallmon Presidential Papers, Carleton College Archives.

29 Merrill Jarchow, *Donald J. Cowling: Educator, Idealist, Humanitarian* (Northfield, MN: Carleton College, 1974).

30 *Alumni Magazine of Carleton College*, vol. 1 (May 1910).

31 *Alumni Magazine of Carleton College*, vol. 1 (May 1910), 47.

32 Donald Cowling to Norman Patton, 20 January 1912, President's Office Records (Cowling), Carleton College Archives.

33 Norman Patton to Donald Cowling, 4 March 1912, President's Office Records (Cowling), Carleton College Archives.

34 Donald Cowling to Morris Holmes, 4 February 1914, President's Office Records (Cowling), Carleton College Archives.

35 Morris Holmes to Donald Cowling, 28 February 1916, President's Office Records (Cowling), Carleton College Archives.

36 John E. Boodin, "Carleton College," *Alumni Magazine of Carleton College*, vol. VI, no. 4 (February 1916), 129–33.

37 *Carletonian*, March 23, 1915, 1.

38 Morris Holmes to Donald Cowling, 8 April 1916, President's Office Records (Cowling), Carleton College Archives.

39 Morris Holmes to Donald Cowling, 28 December 1915, President's Office Records (Cowling), Carleton College Archives.

40 Morris Holmes to Donald Cowling, 12 January 1916, President's Office Records (Cowling), Carleton College Archives.

41 Donald Cowling to Morris Holmes, 2 August 1915, President's Office Records (Cowling), Carleton College Archives.

42 Lauren Soth, *Architecture at Carleton* (Northfield, MN: Carleton College, 2002), 5.

43 Application for entering the Skinner Memorial Chapel on the National Register of Historic Places, prepared by Britta Bloomberg, April 1981, Chapel files, Carleton College Archives.

44 "Skinner Memorial Chapel Dedicated Sunday Morning," *Carletonian*, October 11, 1916, 1.

45 *Northfield News*, October 13, 1916, 1.

46 *Carletonian*, October 11, 1916.

47 Donald Cowling to Raymond Flinn, 10 October 1916, President's Office Records (Cowling), Carleton College Archives.

48 Charles Mierow, "College Chapel Buildings in America," paper presented at the 1930 Association of American Colleges (AAC) conference by Charles Mierow, president of Colorado College and formerly professor of biography at Carleton, Carleton College Archives.

49 *Carleton College News Bulletin*, vol. 2, no. 3 (December 1919), 3.

50 *Alumni Magazine of Carleton College*, vol. 2, no. 3 (December 1911), 269.

51 Donald Cowling, "The Pilgrims of Today," undated speech, Carleton College Archives.

52 This account of the conflict with the Reverend Riley and the Minnesota Baptists comes from an article in the *Carleton Voice*, reprinted on the Carleton Sesquicentennial website in 2016.

53 *Fiftieth Annual Catalog of Carleton College for the Academic Year 1916–17* (Northfield, MN: Carleton College), 7–22.

54 Ibid., 21–22.

55 Ibid., 24.

56 *Catalog of Carleton College for the Academic Year 1940–41* (Northfield, MN, Carleton College), 40.

57 Jeanne Halgren Kilde, *Nature and Revelation: A History of Macalester College* (Minneapolis: University of Minnesota Press, 2010).

58 Merrill Jarchow, *Donald J. Cowling: Educator, Idealist, Humanitarian* (Northfield, MN: Carleton College, 1974), 117.

59 Ibid., 119.

60 Leal Headley and Merrill Jarchow, *Carleton: The First Century* (Northfield, MN: Carleton College, 1966), 164.

61 *Carleton College News Bulletin*, vol. 1, no. 3 (February 1919).

62 Ibid., 6–7.

63 Ibid., 18–19.

64 "Faculty Committee on Religious Activity (CRA) Report, 1927–28," Cowling Presidential Papers, Carleton College Archives.

65 "Faculty Committee on Religious Activity (CRA) Report, 1942–43," Cowling Presidential Papers, Carleton College Archives.

66 Op. cit., Jarchow, *Donald J. Cowling*, 127.

67 *Fiftieth Annual Catalog of Carleton College for the Academic Year 1916–17* (Northfield, MN: Carleton College), 61.

68 "Faculty Committee on Religious Activity (CRA) Report, 1926–27," Cowling Presidential Papers, Carleton College Archives.

69 *Algol* (Northfield, MN: Carleton College, 1936), 227.

70 *Algol* (Northfield, MN: Carleton College, 1915), 169.

71 *The Carletonian*, Vol. 55, No. 3, October 10, 1934, 1.

72 "Statement Regarding Religious Interests and Activities at Carleton," in "Religious Activities" file, Cowling Presidential Papers, Carleton College Archives.

73 *Carleton College Bulletin: Seventy-Ninth Annual Catalog* (Northfield, MN: Carleton College, 1946), 89, Carleton College Archives.

74 Eric Hillemann, *A Beacon So Bright: The Life of Laurence McKinley Gould* (Northfield, MN: Carleton College, 2012), 319.

75 *Carleton College Bulletin: Seventy-Ninth Annual Catalog* (Northfield, MN: Carleton College, 1946), 91, Carleton College Archives.

76 *The Voice of the Carleton Alumni*, September 1946.

77 Philip Phenix, "Report of the Counselor in Religion, 1947–48," Gould Presidential Papers, Carleton College Archives.

78 Ibid., 7.

79 Ibid., 3–6.

80 Philip Phenix to Lawrence M. Gould, 20 April 1950, Gould Presidential Papers, Carleton College Archives.

81 Philip Phenix to Lawrence M. Gould, 28 December 1950, Gould Presidential Papers, Carleton College Archives.

82 Seymour A. Smith, "Survey of Provisions for Religion at Carleton College 1951–1952," in the "Religious Activities" file, Box 4, Gould Presidential Papers, Carleton College Archives.

83 Ibid., 6.

84 *Carleton College Bulletin: Eighty-Fourth Annual Catalog* (Northfield, MN: Carleton College, 1951), Carleton College Archives.

85 Lawrence M. Gould to James Flint, 1 April 1948, the "Flint" file, Gould Presidential Papers, Carleton College Archives.

86 James Flint, "The Report to the President from the Dean of the Chapel, 1948–49," 4, in the "Religious Activities" file, Gould Presidential Papers, Carleton College Archives.

87 Lawrence M. Gould to James Flint, drafted 21 November 1949, notated "not sent," in the "Flint" file, Gould Presidential Papers, Carleton College Archives.

88 Lawrence M. Gould to James Flint, drafted 13 January 1950, notated "not sent," in the "Flint" file, Gould Presidential Papers, Carleton College Archives.

89 Lawrence M. Gould to James Flint, 22 February 1950, in the "Flint" file, Gould Presidential Papers, Carleton College Archives.

90 Lawrence M. Gould to Laird Bell, 18 May 1951, in the "Flint" file, Gould Presidential Papers, Carleton College Archives.

91 *The Voice of the Carleton Alumni*, September 1953, 7.

92 David Stowe, "Faith in Action on a College Campus," *Advance, the National Journal of Congregational Christian Churches*, vol. 147, no. 22 (November 30, 1955), 5–6.

93 This is David Maitland's recollection, taken from an interview transcript in the Carleton College Oral History Collection. The interview was conducted by Joan Reitz on May 22 and 26, 1993.

94 Ian Barbour and David Maitland, "Religion at Carleton," *The Voice of the Carleton Alumni*, April 1958, 3–4.

95 "Carleton Chaplain Must Be Minister, Teacher, Adviser," *Minneapolis Tribune*, January 2, 1961, in "Chaplain's Office" files, Carleton College Archives.

96 *The Chapel and Religion at Princeton*, a brochure for students sent by Professor Henry Woodward to President Lawrence M. Gould, in the "Religious Affairs Committee" file, Gould Presidential Papers, Carleton College Archives.

97 "Religion and the Liberal Arts" in *Beloit College Trends*, a publication of Beloit College, Beloit, Wisconsin, 1962. Sent by Ralph Henry to President Lawrence M. Gould, in the "Religious Activities Committee" file, Gould Presidential Papers, Carleton College Archives.

98 Ian Barbour and David Maitland, "Religion at Carleton," *The Voice of the Carleton Alumni*, April 1958, 3.

99 John Nason, "The Religious Requirement: An Historical Perspective," *Carleton Voice*, March 1964, 12.

100 "Unanimous Proposal and Recommendations of the Faculty Committee on Religious Affairs," sent to the Carleton Trustees, May 1964. In the "Faculty Committee on Religious Affairs" file in the John Nason Presidential Collection, Carleton College Archives.

101 "The Aims of Carleton College" was written by Bardwell Smith and the Faculty Committee on Religious Affairs and attached to and submitted with a "Unanimous Proposal and Recommendations" to the Board of Trustees in May 1964. In the "Faculty Committee on Religious Affairs" file in the John Nason Presidential Collection, Carleton College Archives.

102 John Nason, "Memorandum to All Carleton Alumni," June 24, 1964, sent to individual alumni, in the John Nason Presidential Collection, Carleton College Archives.

103 "Discussion of the Decision: The Religious Requirement," *Carleton Voice*, September 1964, 14–25.

104 Ibid., 15.

105 Ibid., 19–20.

106 John Nason, "1963–1964 Report of the President to Trustees, Alumni, and Friends," October 1964, Carleton College Archives.

107 David Maitland, "Critical Loyalty," *Carleton Voice*, January 1970, 15, 17. An article adapted from a sermon delivered by Maitland at the Sunday Morning Service of October 19, 1969, in Skinner Chapel.

108 "Range of Present Religious Activities: A Preliminary Account of the Work of the Chaplains," March 31, 1965, in the "David Maitland" files in the Chaplain's Office Collection, Carleton College Archives.

109 Joel Tibbets, "Job Description: Assistant Chaplain," dated February 6, 1967, in the Chaplain's Office Collection, Carleton College Archives.

110 Facilities Director Keith Covey, "Chapel Seating Capacity," dated January 29, 1981, memo in the "Skinner Chapel" files, Carleton College Archives.

111 David Maitland, "The Chapel Banners," brochure written in May 1982 and reprinted in 2010, and available in Skinner Chapel.

112 Interview with David Maitland by Joan Reitz, May 22 and 26, 1993. Transcript in the Carleton College Digital Oral History Collection, Carleton College Archives.

113 Ibid., 6–7.

114 David Maitland to Emma Turner, president of the BCOC, memo dated 4 June 1981, "Chaplain's Office" files, Carleton College Archives.

115 "Traditional God 'Reborn' on Campuses," *Northfield News*, December 12, 1978.

116 "The American Freshman: Forty Year Trends," a report of the Cooperative Institutional Research Program, Higher Education Research Institute, UCLA, Los Angeles, April 2007.

117 Robert Edwards to members of the Committee on the Future of the Chaplaincy, February 1985, in the Chaplain's Office Collection, Carleton College Archives.

118 Letter submitted to the Future of the Chaplaincy Committee, May 1985, in the Chaplain's Office Collection, Carleton College Archives.

119 "Report of the Committee on the Future of the Chaplaincy," dated June 10, 1985, submitted to President Edwards, in the "Religious Activity" files of the Edwards Presidential Collection and files from the Chaplain's Office, Carleton College Archives.

120 Ibid., 4.

121 Ibid., 6.

122 Ibid., 8.

123 Ibid., 8–9.

124 "The Future of the Chaplaincy," *Carleton Voice*, Summer 1986, 12.

125 David Maitland, "The Chapel: A Secular Place in Ecclesiastical Garb," *Carletonian*, October 20, 1989.

126 Ibid.

127 Farewells: David Maitland, http://apps.carleton.edu/farewells/?story_id821357.

128 Ibid.

129 Robert Edwards to the Carleton community, dated May 20, 1986, in the "Jewelnel Davis" file, Carleton College Archives.

130 Nancy Ashmore, "Carleton's New Chaplain: A Woman on the Move," *Carleton Voice*, Winter 1987, 32–34.

131 David Porter to Jewelnel Davis, dated 27 May 1987, in the "Chaplain's Office" files, Carleton College Archives.

132 Stephen Lewis to Jewelnel Davis, reappointment letter dated 15 June 1988, in the Lewis Presidential Collection, Carleton College Archives.

133 Richard Crouter to Stephen Lewis, memorandum Re: Jewelnel Davis' Third Year Review, dated 23 September 1989, in the Lewis Presidential Collection, Carleton College Archives.

134 William Wells to Richard Crouter and the Chaplaincy Review Committee, letter dated 17 May 1989, in the "Jewelnel Davis" file in the Lewis Presidential Collection, Carleton College Archives. In the same letter Wells gave Davis a ringing endorsement, writing "If there were a Jewelnel Davis fan club around, I would be honored to serve as president. It is my feeling that her presence at Carleton has been extraordinarily beneficial to all segments of the Carleton community. Her fairness and humanness in dealing with diverse racial groups; her continuous generosity in listening to and discussing serious religious and personal issues with students and faculty; her support of various religious and minority groups including the Carleton Gay-Lesbian Organization — all these commitments and tasks have been carried out by Chaplain Davis with great sensitivity and energy."

135 Stephen Lewis to Faculty and Staff, letter dated 22 June 1989, in the Dean of Students Collection, Carleton College Archives.

136 Stephen Lewis to Jewelnel Davis, letter dated 6 October 1992, in the Lewis Presidential Collection, Carleton College Archives.

137 Stephen Lewis to Students, Faculty, and Staff, a letter dated 14 May 1990, in the Dean of Students Collection, Carleton College Archives.

138 Anonymous Letter to Students, Faculty, and Staff, dated 16 May 1990, in the Dean of Students Collection, Carleton College Archives.

139 "She Ministers to Many Needs," *Northfield News*, 16 February 1994.

140 Ibid.

141 Mark Govoni to Jewelnel Davis, memorandum dated 17 August 1995, in the Dean of Students Collection, Carleton College Archives.

142 Stephen Lewis to Students, Faculty, and Staff, dated 7 March 1996, in the "Jewelnel Davis" file, Carleton College Archives.

143 "Mission, Vision, Values, and Goals," *Carleton College Catalog for 2006–07* (Northfield, MN: Carleton College, 2006–07), 1.

144 Ibid.

145 *Catalog* (Northfield, MN: Carleton College, 1880), 24, Carleton College Archives.

146 Lisa Ebert to Carleton Faculty and Staff, 9 September 1996, "Chaplain's Office" files, Carleton College Archives.

147 "Carleton Names New Chaplain," *Northfield News*, May 30, 1997.

148 "Giving Something More: New Chaplain at Carleton College Wears Many Hats," *Northfield News*, November 7, 1997.

149 *Skinner Memo*, October 1997, "Chaplain's Office" files, Carleton College Archives.

150 *Skinner Memo*, September 1998, "Chaplain's Office" files, Carleton College Archives.

151 "Carleton Hosting Six-Week Diversity Series," *Northfield News*, March 31, 2001.

152 "The Office of the Chaplain at Carleton College: Annual Report. March 15, 2002," provided to the author by Chaplain Carolyn Fure Slocum. The description of the chaplaincy that follows was taken from the 2001–2, 2008–09, and 2013–14 Chaplain Office Annual Reports.

153 "Keeping the Faith at Carleton," a publication of the history of Soul Zone Ministries, compiled and edited by Deb Hvass and Nikki Reich, Northfield, MN. Copy in the Chaplain's Office.

154 "The Office of the Chaplain at Carleton College: Annual Report. July 1, 2009," 16, provided to the author by Chaplain Carolyn Fure Slocum.

155 Taken from remarks by President Steve Poskanzer at the Chapel's Centennial Dinner, Sept 29, 2016.

Index

of names, places, and organizations

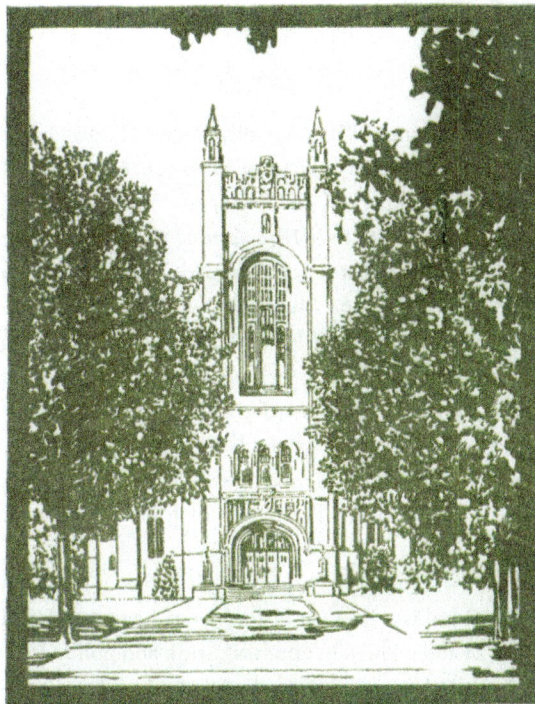

Photo and Illustration Credits

Historical images and photos of religious activities are courtesy of the Carleton College Archives and the Office of the Chaplain, who provided a glimpse into this little-photographed aspect of campus life.

Cover photos and photos on pages v, 21, 22, 27, 28, 85, 113, 115, 117, 122, 128, and 130, and stained glass illustrations and initials are by Mark F. Heiman.

Illustrations on pages 2, 33, 43, 56, 72, 97, and 135 are student-created art from the Carleton College yearbook, the *Algol*.

Historian Bruce William Colwell has researched, authored, and published four local histories: *Everlasting Influences: The Centennial History of the Northfield Carnegie Public Library 1910-2010; Learning to Make the World a Better Place: The History of the Prairie Creek Community School, 1983-2015; The Enduring Good We Do Today: A History of the Northfield Public Library, 1998-2016;* and *This Noble Edifice: A History of Religious and Spiritual Life at Carleton, 1866-2016.* He also has four more projects in progress: histories of the Northfield Arts Guild, the Northfield Public Schools, and The Northfield City Hospital, and a history of the Presidency of John Nason at Carleton College.

Colwell holds a B. A. in history from Lawrence University (1972) and a Ph.D. in administration and policy studies from the Northwestern University School of Education and Social Policy (1988).

Prior to becoming a local historian, Colwell worked in higher education, amassing more than thirty years of administrative experience as an associate dean of students at Lawrence University and Northwestern University, and senior associate dean of students at Carleton College. While at Carleton, Colwell wrote the college's first Residential Life Handbook, *The Family Guide to Carleton College,* and the *Senior Year Experience Guide 2009.*

Colwell has served as a member and president of the Northfield Public Library Board and the Northfield Historical Society Board. He lives in Northfield.

CPSIA information can be obtained
at www.ICGtesting.com
Printed in the USA
LVOW02s0211071016
507738LV00001B/1/P

9 780961 391133